She has a Secret

Douglas Weiss, Ph.D.

Requests for information should be addressed to:

Discovery Press
P.O. Box 51055, Colorado Springs, CO 80949
719-278-3708

Library of Congress Cataloging-in-Publication Data
Weiss, D. She Has A Secret: Understanding Female Sexual Addiction
2nd Edition/ D. W. Weiss p. cm.
Discovery Press, 2008
ISBN 1-881292-58-4

1. Women's Issues 2. Sexuality 3. Sex Addiction 99-97796 CIP

Cover and Interior design by Janelle Evangelides

Printed in the United States of America

Dedication

To the women who have had the secret
and to those who have gone
beyond their secrets to healing

＊This book is much less threatening to me b/c it is so similar to male sex addiction, but it is not hurting me (PTSD) I don't take it so personally now - its not promoting the lie that all men are sex addicts. Its helping me see a more balanced perspective -

Table of Contents

Introduction
From the Heart

In the following pages you are about to meet some of the most courageous women in America. They are women who are in various stages of sexual addiction recovery. Sex addiction has led them down a trail of endless, anonymous encounters and affairs destroying themselves and their families.

A female sex addict often has a secret sexual life, with herself or with others. She uses sex to medicate past pains such as abuse or neglect. She may also use sex to cope with her present life-style. Either way she begins to spiral down where the "fix" becomes more important to her than the people she truly loves.

Addiction has been a part of American culture for a very long time. Since 1930, we as a culture looked at alcoholism as an addiction and it was often addressed as a "man's disease." Then Betty Ford broke the gender stereotype of this disease. In the 1980s we started identifying and treating sexual addiction. This too, until recently had been addressed by our culture as a "male" problem. The women you are about to meet shatter that paradigm. Sexual addiction is not only cross-cultural it crosses gender lines as well.

Allow me tell you about the women who participated in our survey and shared their stories to further the understanding of sexual addiction. They are not crack cocaine junkies selling themselves

it's about pain for the sex addict - torment
mostly abused

for sex. Rather these are doctor's wives, attorneys, florists, sales people, stay-at-home moms and even church attendees. The woman addicted to sex can be almost any woman. She lives a secret, double life and only she knows the pain that is involved. This book is designed to help her with the pain of her secret.

The twenty-four women participating in our study share their secrets in hope of helping others get free from their own secrets. The following statistics will help you identify who these women are that have contributed to our study on female sex addicts. Fifty-six percent of the women respondents were married, 22% were divorced and 22% were single. Fifty-eight percent are full-time employees, 29% stay-at-home mothers and 16% were business owners. If she has children, she has an average of two children. Fifty-eight percent are mothers. They also reported that as an average they felt they have been addicted to sex for 21 years. Many have been abused throughout their lives and will give you their true stories on the following pages right from their heart. It is all of our hopes that you will be encouraged enough through this book to begin to heal from any secrets in your life.

56% married   58% Full-time employees

22% divorced   29% stay at home moms

22% single   16% business owners

58% mothers

Secret Fantasy

Sexual addiction entangles the lives of many women who have secrets. In the chapters ahead of you, numerous men will share, from their hearts, diverse sexual secrets that have greatly affected many aspects of their lives. Each of their stories will vary from woman to woman so every chapter will open another door where secrets have lurked. These secrets have been gathered and shared so that others can better understand sexual addiction firsthand, along with the dire need for recovery. The secrets now shared in this first chapter will be that of the secret of fantasy.

I tend to fantasize during masturbation. I understand that when men fantasize, they can visualize a specific woman, her specific features, etc. But with me, my fantasies never include a specific person. I find myself longing intensely for the sex act and the physical parts which a man provides for that. Any man will do. I don't care whose face is attached at the other end of the body. I usually am imagining that I am doing the sex act with my husband. Of course, since I have never had a husband, this means I am still hoping for a future husband.
--Abby   lonely

I find I tend to fantasize more when I'm in emotional pain or want to avoid a difficult situation. --Constance

emotional pain, avoidance

Fantasy is one of the biggest parts of my addiction and this is the area where I struggle most in my sobriety. This is definitely harder to get sobriety from than acting out. I began fantasizing from the time I started masturbating. --Debra

I have used persistent abusive fantasies to begin to reconstruct a picture of what happened to me as a child. It has only been in the last few months—after about six years of recovery—that I have begun to see masturbation as something harmful to me. --Evelyn

Fantasy is a big problem in my addiction. I have always thought of people other than the person I am with sexually at the time. I started getting physically attracted to boys and started thinking of them when I masturbated. That was my first encounter with fantasy. I have a very difficult time getting aroused since then without fantasy. My sexual world revolves around who I have seen in a movie that day or even in real life.

I can now see how having a healthy fantasy world, about the person one is dating at the time, can be very exciting. I believe fantasizing about others (if one is in a monogamous relationship) is very harmful to one's self and the relationship. (I feel it is one of the building blocks to cheating.)

Healthy

In my recovery, I am trying to reprogram my thought process to more real life-like fantasy about my husband. I am re-training my brain to see the other people as damaging and my husband as exciting. (He really is too). --Julie

Fantasy affected me in only a few ways and it usually stemmed from one or more guys promising me the world and telling me everything I wanted to hear. --Laura

Fantasy has played a huge role in my addiction. At age 11, I started my menstrual cycle. My mother never spoke to me about the changes that would occur in me. She might have tried, but in any case, I had feelings I did not know what to do with.

Since I had already come in contact with pornography and adult novels, I was able to take in the pictures and the words to feed my sexual fantasies. I mentally had sex for years before acting out physically. The first time I had sex was when I was 14 with a boy the same age. It didn't even come close to what I had in my mind.

As the addiction progressed in my life, I began living out my fantasies. The only sexual satisfaction I have ever had was when I had sex with other sex addicts or in illicit relationships. I think what triggered the enticement to illicit relationships was adult novels of deceit and soap operas. It first started in a two-year relationship I had when I was 19. He was of a different race so my parents forbid me to see him. I lied every time I left the house about where I was going and whom I was going to be with. I learned to keep my relationship with my boyfriend separate from my relationship with my family. Two years later my parents caught me in an enormous lie. They told me if he meant that much to me that they would no longer forbid me to see him. I broke up with him 3 weeks later. This pattern progressed over the years into my adult life. I would maintain a "committed" relationship and act out sexually with others. I never imagined that I would continue this behavior into my first marriage. I did, and it destroyed it. --Tina

Fantasy is something I have always struggled with. Looking back, I am not sure I ever approached life in any other frame of mind. I was sure there was "romance" somewhere, but found that the only way to get near it was to offer my body-only to find disappointment once again.

This became a real problem when I was in college. I realized that I saw my sex as sort of a power over men. I never allowed myself to be hurt. But there were countless men. And each one undoubtedly DID hurt me. Denying it didn't stop the pain. Marriage was disappointing to me because I wasn't the center of attention - even with sex, like I thought I would be. I craved the excitement of "forbidden love." I devoured books and movies with that theme behind them. I toyed with it in everything I did. Even going shopping I found my-

excitement of the forbidden

deceit

* power over men - protection But still got hurt

Needed to be center of attention Reality-boring

excitement of forbidden love

self eyeing other men and fantasizing about them wanting me. Nothing was taboo in fantasy.

I guess it all boils down to wanting attention. In all my fantasies, I am the center of everyone's attention. Being submissive in the fantasy relieved me of the responsibility of what I was doing. I see things so differently now. I see that I am not in that cloud anymore. I didn't even realize I was in one.

Addiction will need more + more I had one on-line lover that I was with 3 years - he is the one I tried to meet. He was really into things like bondage and mild mutilation like needles and injections. I would take pictures of myself for him with a needle or two if I could manage to get them in. I found that there was kind of a rush with the sight of them once they were in. I know he would have taken it too far for me had we been able to meet. That scares me now, but I was in such a state of fantasy then that I thought it was erotic to be in pain. Weird! --Rhonda

My fantasy goes hand in hand with acting out and it feels like an insurmountable mountain to climb. I'm scared, frightened, alone, and scattered going through this phase of recovery. This is going to be difficult to say the very least. --Francine

So sad! Much of my fantasy has centered around being hurt and/or raped which I know is deeply rooted in my sexual abuse. This is both my addiction and abuse, entwined. --Margaret

The first fantasy experience I recall was when I began masturbating at age 12. I typically had fantasies of unknown males. I recycled 2 or 3 fantasies. The strongest one being that I was in an Indian tribe being initiated for sexual relations — come to think of it, 2 of my fantasies were "Indian Tribe" related. I used to read "National Geographic" and believe this is where the fantasies were born. They were definitely me being submissive, and generally with a group of men.

As I got a bit older, the submissive fantasies continued — rape (though not torture) was a theme (still is). Group sex with others dominating me are also strong with me. Fantasy is definitely a major part of my addiction, as it has affected all areas of my life. Every relationship I have had I have expressed this fantasy of sub-missiveness — some men have taken on the dominant role and some have not. Not until the most recent relationship (my affair), did some s/m get involved. I never really thought that my fanta-sies were "bad." I never tried to stop or control them.

Not until I went into treatment did I realize the damage and the danger my fantasies were putting me into. I was abused both physically and sexually by my father (sexually, both overtly and covertly). I did not realize that I was just reliving my "trauma." With my attempts to resolve my stuff, I was continuing to reinjure myself in the process. I used to think that any sexual behavior be-tween two consenting adults was okay as long as it didn't harm anyone else. I do not think that anymore. I WAS HARMING MY-SELF EVERY TIME I ENGAGED IN MY FANTASIES WHETHER OR NOT THEY WERE ACTUALLY ACTED OUT IN MY HEAD OR FOR REAL (and in the end, they were acted out more for real than in my head). I still struggle withhe fantasy stuff. I never really understood how women could just "get off" on the Harlequin Romance fantasy stuff (making love on the beach with the man of your dreams). I still do not know what is okay or not okay. I just know that if I am not IN THE PRESENT in my fantasy (in my mind) then it probably is not okay for me. Fantasy has the ability to take me far, far away from ME. I am able to really disengage and disconnect from real-ity. For me, that is not a good place to be. For me, it is like a major drug high. So my rule of thumb: STAY TOTALLY PRESENT. I am not perfect, but I do believe in not beating myself up about it (had enough of that in my life from others). --Kittie

Subconsciously re-harming self over & over.

Healthy - Stay in the present

The fantasy was to escape the pain. I remember it especially af-fecting me in my teenage years as I led a double life - one of this high achieving girl academically - the other of a fantasy world of sex, orgies, etc. I did not date in high school and never had a boyfriend ether. I was withdrawn, shy, insecure, unsure of myself. There were a lot of repressed feelings inside of me. -- Debra

escape pain

The fantasy world is an incredibly powerful and very real component in the life of a woman addicted to sex. Although she may be able to function as a wife, mother, and co-worker she is often involved in a fantasy world where she has much more control than the real world she actually lives and functions in.

[handwritten: escape to reality" feel "fake empowerment - which leaves her more empty. a "fake" empowerment]

This fantasy world is different for each female sex addict. As you have read in the stories above, some preferred to escape into a nirvana where they are loved and cared for with a magical lover who knows exactly what to say, and knows where exactly to touch. This reliable world is magical and never disappoints her, unlike the real world.

Some women caught up in the fantasy world are reenacting in their fantasies to events that have happened in their past such as sexual traumas or rapes. Their fantasies are an attempt at obtaining mastery and control over past pain. Their fantasies can be as simple as performing a similar sex act on someone else of the same gender as their past perpetrator. Sometimes the fantasy re-enactment is having their sexual partner performing the sex act on them, as was done when they were a victim. This is a way for them to not be the victim again in their fantasy world.

Although the fantasies vary from woman to woman, it can be strongly hypothesized that the majority often do use some type of fantasy as the previous stories unveiled. Fantasy is a big part of the acting out behaviors for a female sex addict. When she is having sex with a partner, her mind, heart, and spirit are often disconnected and somewhere else.

Upon reviewing our study of women addicted to sex, we have learned much about the role of fantasy. The first inquiry about sexual fantasy revealed the type of fantasy they had in the midst of their addiction. Their responses stated that 57% of their sexual fantasies were degrading to themselves. Thirty percent stated that their sexual fantasies during their addiction were neutral (not degrading, nor nurturing) and only 13% in our study had fantasies that were nurturing to themselves.

This same study examined who they fantasized about. Fifty-nine percent stated that the sexual fantasies in their addiction were about someone they knew in their real world. Twenty-two percent stated that their sexual fantasies were about people they did not know, and 19% stated their fantasy was with pornography they had viewed.

Further inquiry into the fantasy world of women addicted to sex revealed who was pursuing or being pursued in their fantasy. Forty-six percent reported that they were being pursued during the sexual fantasy, and 18% stated they were the pursuer.

Thirty-six percent stated that they equally pursue and are pursued in their sexual fantasy.

It is interesting to note that 60% stated that in their fantasy they were mostly submissive. Thirteen percent stated that they were the dominant partner. Twenty-seven percent stated that they were equally dominant and submissive in their sexual fantasies, in the midst of their sexual addiction life-style.

The last question specific to fantasy in the study of women addicted to sex was the amount of time they were in fantasy while acting out with their sexual partner. Thirty-eight percent of the women studied stated that 80% or more of the time they were sexual with someone, they were also in a fantasy state. Five percent stated that they were 50% or more of the time in a fantasy state while with their sexual partner. Thirty-eight percent, however, stated that they were in a fantasy state less than 50% of the time. Nineteen percent stated that during their sexual activity with their partner they were never in a fantasy state.

Occasionally the woman addicted to sex may select another sexual addict as her sexual partner and he also may be in a fantasy state during their sex act. This would mean that, emotionally, both are not having sex with each other. If both are disconnected and in a fantasy state neither are getting any emotional connection from each other during the sexual act, both would probably feel unfulfilled from this union.

Sex addiction- no emotional connection b/c both in their own fantasies.

The power of fantasy can kick in at any stage of the sexual act. Fantasy is a large part of the lure of her sexual addiction and keeps it fueled. Fantasy is the primary secret in the life of a female sex addict.

Secret Self Sex

The secret of self sex otherwise know as masturbation, may be one of the darkest secrets of all for the woman addicted to sex. For some, self sex is the totality of their sexual addiction. For others it just fills in the gap between episodes of acting out with other partners. Either way, self sex is rarely talked about. In this unusually candid chapter, women will share about when this sexual behavior emerged in their life. You will read each of their stories which reveal the starting point for this behavior as being in childhood, in adulthood, or a result of past sexual abuse. Regardless of when this behavior started, you will realize self sex has been a dark secret for many sexually-addicted woman.

It started at age 14 and was the result of my accidental discovery of my sexual functions. During the earlier stage of my life, I probably did it about once a month. Gradually it increased, and at age 17, I was counting 10 times a day. During adulthood, for roughly 20 years, I have been masturbating an average of between three and five times every day. I think that masturbation is my problem. I figure I have had about 50,000 incidents of this behavior in my life. But with men, perhaps 50 incidents. I still have problems with masturbation and I have not been able to stop it. I am in recovery groups, but some would say I'm not in recovery because I still act out this way.
--Abby

So sad – masturbation is now controlling her, she is not controlling it.

I began masturbating at an extremely young age. My patterns were constant and ritualistic. As a child I would masturbate right before I went to sleep at night. It increased to the point that I couldn't sleep unless I had an orgasm at night. This continued through childhood and adolescence, progressing to the morning as well. It got to the point where I needed an orgasm to wake me up so I could get out of bed. Throughout my childhood my family was very shaming about "IT" and so "IT" was considered a bad and terrible thing. My parents would humiliate and embarrass me, catching me all the time on purpose, then pretending they didn't know what I was doing. I felt spied on to some degree. The whole thing was very sick and deceptive, and only drove me to do "IT" more. I felt like was constantly keeping it a secret, hence the start of my double life.
--Barbara

I began masturbating at about age 13. After viewing pornography for the first few times, I began to explore, discovering this new way to take care of my own needs. This has been a major part of my addiction which mainly consisted of porn, fantasy and masturbation. I have not achieved sobriety with these issues. I have with porn, but this has been much harder, although the frequency has lessened for most of the time. For me, masturbating seemed to be my only outlet, my own private secret, and mine alone. I've never drunk, smoked, done drugs, or even had intercourse. I was a classic overachiever and because of my faith, I knew there were certain things I could not do. Masturbation seemed the perfect mask of choice. One thing I've learned, masturbation is guilt free sex that ISN'T guilt free! I still struggle with this. I hate that I do, but as the shame and guilt lessen, as I recover from my addictive behavior and my abuse (which are intermingled), the struggle gets easier.
--Margaret

I started masturbating when I was 11. I loved the feeling of masturbation and I would fantasize about being with a man (or boy). I continued to masturbate or have sex each week, until I was in my thirties when I got sober from alcohol and drugs. I masturbated in my 2nd marriage when I was sexually anorexic with my husband.

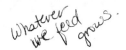
Whatever we feed grows.

Using masturbation as a way to escape or avoid my feelings is using it addictively. In sobriety I found that masturbating on a regular basis keeps the craving going so I have abstained. --Constance

I probably started masturbating around 8 years old. When I was younger I fantasized about my abuse when I masturbated. I then moved to reading romantic novels with very explicit sexual passages. Fantasy is a major part of masturbation for me. I masturbated almost nightly from age 8-18. When I converted to Christianity I stopped because I felt like it was sinful. During my teenage years, I felt I led this double life and hated all the fantasies and masturbation I did. I felt dirty and bad about it. During my 17th year of marriage I only resorted to masturbation when my husband was absent. Being the wife of a minister, I still associated it with being sinful and wrong. After my husband abandoned me, I used masturbation on a constant basis to get through the withdrawal from daily sex with him. I used a vibrator a lot during those years. In my last relationship of 3½ years, I used masturbation a lot as my partner was insensitive to my needs. I placed this on my bottom line just over 1 month ago so I am just beginning to address this issue. --Debra

I have usually not been able to masturbate, or pleasure myself without having a fantasy, which usually involves either a man I'm interested in, or what I consider an abusive fantasy—about a young girl seduced by older men and/or women. --Evelyn

Masturbation began in my 20's during college. I thought it was okay to do it since there was release and feelings of euphoria, and there wasn't another person involved in this scenario. I was fascinated with thinking about oral sex. (No, I was not sexually or physically abused as a child.) To this day I do not know why this intrigued me so very much. I did not know this was the beginning of an addictive cycle. Again, I thought it was safe, okay, and did not involve others. My own little pleasure, all to myself.

I am just beginning to address this behavior in recovery. I know it is all consuming and when I do not have a partner present, it becomes foremost in anything I plan. Maybe it will help other women to know they are not alone in this struggle. --Francine

I frequently masturbate whether I am in a relationship or not, usually several times a week. Sometimes several times, in a day.--Gail

Masturbation started for me on a really regular basis at age 15. I masturbated by myself and with boyfriends on a regular basis as a way to avoid intercourse. The habit continued into adulthood and marriage. It progressed into pornography at age 15, with mostly magazines and video's and xxx theaters as an adult. It felt good and I didn't have to have sex or let anyone close to me. This behavior is a major part of my addiction. It helps me to shut off and avoid life. I started addressing this in recovery a couple of years ago. It is very difficult to admit and face. I still have not overcome this behavior, but I have learned that if I stay connected to other people with phone and meetings, and I pray everyday, the desire to act out is not as strong. Above all I have to be honest with my sponsor and therapist about acting out. NO SECRETS! --Heidi

I started masturbating as a child through my father's abuse. He taught me how to masturbate by using it to meet his own sexual gratification. Later, I began to masturbate by myself as a way to make the pain go away and relax. Especially during adolescence it increased to a daily routine of escape to avoid the pain of my sexual abuse. I began to masturbate more than once daily. It became out of control and was a way to deal with the sexual abuse. In looking at my adulthood I see masturbation as a way of avoiding the pain. --Ivette

I was taught masturbation (digital, water, and vibrator) by a girl several years older than me. I was about 5 years old when she started touching me when I would stay the night with her. I masturbated a lot (two or three times a week) through my school years. I always did it secretively. Since I started dating, I masturbated to fantasies about someone other than the person I was dating at the time. I don't personally masturbate now. (I have masturbated alone about 10 times in 6 years). --Julie

I started using masturbation at age 11. After being sexually abused on nearly an every weekend basis by my perpetrators from age five, I turned to masturbation as they decided I was getting too old for their play. I pursued them for a couple years, yet turned to masturbation to fill the void they left, fantasizing they were there. After a couple of years it became less and less, finally stopping at about the age of 14. I felt it was wrong, and was tired of hiding and feeling the shame and guilt. --Monica

I began masturbating at the age of 12 — I don't really recall where the idea came from. Though I didn't feel guilty about doing it, I didn't know what the orgasms were doing to my body. I thought I was hurting my body with the orgasmic contractions. I bargained with myself at that age that I would only have 500 orgasms before I would stop masturbating. Of course, though I did keep track, I never stuck to the bargain. I did lots of porn reading at that point (father's collection).

I really wasn't into it, I just liked looking at nude bodies. I also fantasized about being taken advantage of (me being submissive). I masturbated probably 4-5 times a week. I remember doing it in the morning and at night when I was feeling anxious, lonely, or bored. I had a boyfriend from the age of 13 onward — I did not have sex until the age of 16.

I have masturbated constantly since the age of 12, whether or not I was in a relationship. All of my relationships were aware of my habit (and encouraged it). I would have to say now that masturbation is a major part of my addiction. I say that because it really takes me away, I feel drugged, I can't have an orgasm unless I either am looking at porn (and that has been progressively perverse), or am thinking about submissive fantasies. I masturbate objectifying others, mostly. But other deviant porn interests me, too. Sometimes I didn't really want to masturbate, but knew that the action of it would take my mind away temporarily. I used to masturbate after having sex with someone that didn't really care for me as a soothing effect for myself.

I had a very difficult time with abstinence surrounding my masturbation. But I do have to say that abstinence for a period of time (90 days for me) was probably the best thing I could have done for myself. I really learned what the behavior was from and when I wanted to act out with masturbation. I was forced to take a look at what was behind the feeling. I learned that I dealt with stress, insecurity, loneliness, conflict, and bad feelings with acting out. Masturbation was my coping mechanism, like a drug. The 90 days was painful, but necessary and very healing. I would say that even if someone didn't want to erase masturbation out of their life forever, at least they should take a look at what is behind it. I do have to admit I have slipped back into the old way of masturbating behavior described previously. I am not really happy with myself about this, though I am not back into my old, other acting-out behaviors. Masturbation seems to be the last behavior I am having a difficult time stopping. --Kittie

After about 10 years of marriage I resumed masturbating. I am not sure exactly why, except I was not happy. When I tried abstaining from masturbation, I thought of having an affair. I continued masturbating about once or twice a month. I had a one-night stand every few years. After 20 years of this cycle, I began masturbating on a daily basis. I told my husband and sometimes he watched. Masturbation lost its edge and affairs became my main course. Eventually we divorced. Masturbation became my best friend. I escaped with it. I felt comforted, safe and alive. I fantasized I was with whomever, wherever I wanted. I was lost in it. I made time alone. I sent my kids to Grammy's. I left work early. I stayed up late. After about 3 months it lost some of its edge. I needed a stronger fix, more "toys," variety. I had a toy bag I hid from my kids. I knew it was wrong, abusive, and becoming out of control. I went to dating and hoped to cut back on the time I spent masturbating. I exchanged one escape with another, still getting that fix.

After I got into recovery, my bottom line was no sex outside my committed relationship. Masturbation was not on the list. I was not ready to give everything up! I soon learned that I was either going into recovery or not - no half measures. --Monica

I started masturbating at a very early age, 3 or 4 years old. I don't remember how or why I started, only that it felt very good and often looked forward to bedtime as opposed to not wanting to go to bed, or nap, previously. I believe I did it at least once a night with fantasy all through childhood and continued after marriage. It peaked in my mid-thirties, at times I would masturbate as many as five times in one day. It has gradually tapered off starting around age 40, to once or twice a week. --Yvonne

As these stories clearly identify, self sex is a common practice of women addicted to sex. The early onset of masturbation is the cornerstone of women addicted to sex. It is usually one of the first consistent sexual behaviors that a very young or teenaged, female sex addict can participate in at almost anytime. The frequency of masturbation was a question in our study and the answer follows.

My masturbation pattern throughout my addiction has been:

46%	very consistent, 3+ times a week.
12.5%	consistent, 1-2 times a week.
12.5%	once every two weeks.
12%	monthly.
4%	less than quarterly.
4%	only in binges.
9%	does not apply

In our research study, we did not ask about self sex being acted out multiple times in one day however as you have read in the previous stories this is definitely a factor for many. Our study pursued the issue of self sex further to reveal how they masturbated. The results to this question follow.

28%	Digitally
30%	Objects
20%	Dildos
15%	Running water of some type
7%	Other

I felt this information was especially important for female sex addicts who may be reading these pages. They may take some comfort in knowing that they are not the only one masturbating in this manner.

While counseling with female sex addicts for many years, I have found that a majority of these women have shame and/or guilt concerning masturbation. Both the female client, and even many therapists counseling these women, fall into the trap where they stereotype that men masturbate but women don't. Thus the female sex addict often doesn't get her masturbation issue addressed during treatment because the issue doesn't come up.

Delving further into our study of self sex, we discovered that 50% of our respondents stated that self sex involved mostly fantasy (80% or more of the time). Thirty-six percent stated this behavior involved some fantasy (50-80% of the time). Only 14% stated that masturbation involved little fantasy (less than 50% of the time). No one in our study stated that masturbation did not involve fantasy. Masturbation is a critical issue for most women addicted to sex. The issue of self sex is important to address early in sexual addiction recovery.

When seeing a therapist, the female sex addict needs to be sure to be honest, not only to address the frequency of masturbation and the amount of years this behavior has been a part of her life, but also how primary this sexual behavior is to the addiction.

Many female sex addicts in therapy reveal in the counseling session that they are acting out sexually with men on a regular basis. On the surface it may appear that masturbation is not an issue. Yet upon further investigation, the sexual act with a man only provided the images for a later masturbation event. In recovery, masturbation is usually a primary issue. It is usually the last sexual addictive behavior to go. One reason that this behavior is so difficult to control in recovery is because it was a behavior that started very early in many female sex addicts' lives.

Secondly, the behavior is difficult to control because it bonds the sex addict to the act of masturbation instead of a healthy sexual relational expression of intimacy. The frequency of masturbation, along with the chemical reinforcement the brain receives through this act reinforces this bonding. This will be discussed at greater length in the next chapter.

A third reason this self sex behavior can be difficult to stop is because it is viewed as less important than others she may be involved in. This rationale is much like the alcoholic who stops drinking hard whisky on the weekends, but doesn't see the effects of her daily beer intake, or the pain it is causing in her life and the lives of others. This will become even clearer to you as you read the next section on the "Biological Aspects" of sexual addiction.

In sexual recovery groups taking place across the country, the priority of masturbation varies from group to group. Some groups state that sobriety includes no masturbation while other groups allow you to decide whether masturbation should be a part of your recovery or not.

My encouragement to you is that if masturbation has been a significant part of your addiction then masturbation should be a part of your recovery. I know this will be challenging. Clients at our counseling center who make this a part of their recovery, say that it has been instrumental for them to become whole in other areas of their lives. Choose your journey of recovery wisely and don't be influenced by those who may still be indulging.

Biological Aspects

Just like other addictions, sexual addiction is multifaceted. It isn't caused by any singular reason. Its roots can be found in many possible areas.

Much like alcoholism was in its earlier days, sexual addiction has been viewed as a moral problem. Some think, "If she would just control herself..." Too often sexual addiction has been cast as a character or spiritual problem. Many people have labeled it a psychological problem. The real root of sexual addiction isn't any one factor. And discovering the root to sex addiction requires a thorough study of the possible causes. To begin our search for the cause, let's examine what I call the missing link -- the Biological Aspect.

The Biological Aspect is sometimes the missing piece for women addicted to sex. It offers hope and explanations to those who have searched elsewhere for answers to how their addiction started. For example, many sex addicts have tried spiritual solutions, such as praying ing, without experiencing any improvement in their sexual behavior. Others who have grown up in fairly healthy homes having had no psychological trauma or abuse are confused as to why they are sexually addicted. Sex addicts who have explored these areas with no results find that the biological component is often the missing link they have been searching for.

There are several Biological Aspects of sex addiction. But before we can begin to grapple with the biological and neurological aspects of sex addiction, we first must have a brief discussion about the brain.

The brain is an organ just like the lungs and heart. Organs have needs, including chemical needs that must be met. Endorphins and enkephalins are two of the many chemicals that the brain needs. Everyone has the need for these chemicals. As a part of its developmental tasks, the brain is driven to get this need met. The brain can get these endorphins and enkephalins in several different ways. Running or high aerobic activity can be one of the ways which the brain receives these two chemicals, resulting in what is often called the "runner's high." A lot of research has been done on the runner's high. This "high" feeling is a neurological buzz or a flood of endorphins and enkephalins which I term "brain cookies." The runner gets to a place during her run in which her body is in enough pain that her brain gets flooded with endorphins and enkephalins which together create an opiate-type substance that creates a buzz. Consequently, it is something the brain will begin to want again and again.

The brain can also get these chemical needs met through creativity, expression, intimacy, or connecting with another person. The brain doesn't necessarily distinguish between right and wrong. It is only focused on getting its neurological needs met.

Let's look at these in a paradigm. Picture the brain as having six or seven small pipes through which the endorphin and enkephalin chemicals enter through. The diameter of each pipe determines the quantity of chemicals that flow through it. A pipe with a wide diameter allows more through than a narrow one. Consequently, if we were athletic in our past, that small pipe may be a little wider than others. If we were not very artistic, that pipe would stay small. If we had never had intimacy in our past or present, that pipe would stay very small. When we do become sexual, we send a lot of endorphins and enkephalins to the brain. These chemicals are powerful substances that flood the brain.

Women addicted to sex consistently report that over time, they are sexual many more times than they are artistic, intimate or athletic. And as they continue to grow older, sexual acting out often becomes more and more regular whether it is self sex, sex with others or both. From regularly acting out sexually, that particular pipe can become the greatest way the brain gets its neurological needs met. Now the brain isn't discerning as to whether this pathway is moral or immoral. It is simply an organ that wants its "brain cookies." If acting out sexually is the primary way to get these "cookies," this may be the very reason why so many women sex addicts have been unsuccessful in their recovery treatment. Their problem really isn't all related to abuse, trauma or spirituality. It's biological. Most likely the sex addict hasn't looked at these neurological aspects that often need reconditioning.

Let's consider another paradigm. Let's now say the brain has a new pathway similar to a freshly cut out dirt road. That dirt road, after being traveled on many times becomes a highway. By the time the sex addict comes for counseling, that sexual behavior road or pathway is much like the autobahn in order for her brain to receive its brain cookies.

Acting out sexually has become the primary way she has conditioned her brain to get its chemical needs met. Many sex addicts understand this reality and the repetition of it. Part of their recovery is learning to balance these neurological pathways or dirt roads by adding other healthy activities to their life-style that will also deliver the endorphin and enkephalin chemicals to the brain. This will be an important part of the healing as we talk about re-training the brain in a later chapter in this book.

Neurological Conditioning

Most of us are familiar with the story of Pavlov's dog. You may have learned about classic conditioning in Psych 101. Pavlov's dog was given food after a bell was rung. Over a period of time, the dog connected the bell with the food so much, that when the bell would ring, the dog would begin to salivate -- thus, a biological response. This can also happen with humans. For example, all of us have run out of school when the bell was rung for recess. I can remember sitting in class at school just waiting for that bell to ring. I had a conditioned response to that bell. I knew when the bell rang, I was allowed to get up and go play.

A sex addict's conditioned response works the same way. Their neurological conditioning is incredible. Most sex addicts who have sexual behaviors with others also have some kind of thought patterns to go along with them. I call this an altered state. Conditioning is usually connected to an "altered state." An altered state, otherwise known as fantasy, is a place sex addicts go mentally to escape reality. In this place, a sex addict feels loved, important, and significant. Of course everyone in this fantasy world are objects similar to robots who do and say everything the addict wants them to.

Objects - only to satisfy the addicts needs.

The Neurological Conditioning occurring in this altered state is actually a sexual conditioning because sexual needs are getting met, but only because they are connecting to something else. What the sexual conditioning is connecting to is the altered state experience (*fantasy*) instead of a healthy relational sexual experience.

When the addict goes into the altered state experience, the brain expects and demands a sexual release. This fantasy world begins with many addicts at a young age of 13 or 14 years old. The body will have physiological responses to whatever sexual thoughts are put into the altered state. Many addicts have connected their neurological and biological conditioning to objects that look a certain "*Blonde*" way in their fantasy world. Some have specific preferences such as body types or a particular hair and eye color combination. Whatever fantasies have been put into the altered state, she will pursue it. This is a classic conditioning process.

Before recovery, the woman sex addict went into this altered state thousands and thousands of times during intercourse or while being sexual with herself, because she has conditioned herself to altered-state sex. This is quite different from relational sex. Many women have reported to me that they have had sexual experiences in the altered state thousands of times before they had their first sexual experience with another person. This is why sex addicts get quite angry when they experience resistance from their partner sexually. Their sexual conditioning has been in their altered state, "Whatever I want, I get it whenever I want it." *Huge!* You can see how the neurological conditioning process is a very important part of sexual addiction. *Very immature. Very selfish!*

When the female sex addict is triggered by a fantasy she has put into her altered state, she begins to "sexually salivate," sort of like Pavlov's dog. If muscle bound males are in the sex addict's fantasy world, and she sees one in reality, she will feel pulled in that direction. This is because of her neurological, biological, and sexual conditioning. It is for this reason that early in recovery she must identify her "trigger group," because this specific group of people will solicit a neurological, biological, and sexual response when she is confronted by it. It is not a cognitive response when she spots her trigger group. It often happens in a microsecond and she finds herself in a dilemma. This dilemma has nothing to do with her husband. It has to do with the conditioning she has done to herself over the years.

Neurological conditioning, if not addressed during treatment, can be the fall of many women sex addicts in their recovery. We will talk later about the spiritual and psychological aspects, which can also set up other causes for this behavior. For example, there may not have been intimacy in your family and you were emotionally deprived in childhood. You may have found that acting out sexually was a way of meeting your emotional needs in childhood. While you were acting out sexually, you were beginning to condition yourself neurologically. So even if you address some of the other issues in your treatment, you still have a neurological conditioning aspect that will need to be addressed to achieve sobriety in recovery.

This chapter is just the beginning to understanding this topic. For a deeper understanding, read *Pathways to Pleasure* by Milkman and Sunderworth. I have heard that the brain is the largest sexual organ we have. I have come to the conclusion from the hundreds of sex addicts I have counseled with, that this is true. This reality can not be ignored and must be evaluated and treated for what it is. You may have heard the saying "once an alcoholic, always an alcoholic." This may be more neurological than anything else. The same is true for sexual addiction--the pathway may grow smaller again over a period of time. While we don't have enough information to make this conclusion, we do see people who have longer periods of sobriety, who struggle a lot less. The addict may need to create new pathways, learn to have relational sex, and retrain her brain. She needs to learn how to have her brain become a partner in her recovery, rather than an enemy.

Alcoholics Anonymous has a saying called "Stinking Thinking." I interpret this during recovery as the neurological needs of the brain saying, "What are you doing? We have done this sexual behavior for 35 years. Why stop something that is working?" From a neurological perspective, the brain has developed this particular method to get its needs met. The woman sex addict has reinforced this method by acting out sexually over and over again. The brain can not distinguish whether this is an appropriate or inappropriate method. But the sex addict knows that this method of getting her brain's chemical needs met eventually can become the problem, and that she needs to change her behaviors to recover. If you would like more os the scientific support for the nuerological aspects of this chapter, I would recommend the AASAT DVD on *Masturbation*.

Secret Pictures

It has been presented in the previous chapters some of the various secrets that woman addicted to sex have. In this chapter we will discuss yet another secret they have: pornography. Women addicted to sex vary in their use of pornography and the different types of pictures that are a part of this secret. Nine women will share the effects these pictures had on their lives and the lives of others.

Pornography has been around my house for as long as I can remember. My step-dad always had the picture magazines. That was no big deal to me, they were women anyway. The real problem for me started when I was in Jr. High. I found some pornographic books under the sink in the bathroom. They didn't have pictures, but stories. Sometimes they would have a picture cartoon. I would sit and read those books a lot. I got into a weird fantasy world by reading them and now still have thoughts about them. I can still get aroused (and disgusted) by reading erotica. Anything erotic can get me excited, except pictures of naked men. I never was interested in the "Playgirl" type magazines. I really have a problem with what I like to read. Like I said, it gets me both excited and disgusted at the same time. When I got older (about 23), I got into looking at the women magazines ("Playgirl," "Penthouse," etc.). I don't feel like I'm homosexual; I feel like that is just part of the addiction. I know now that pornography is a problem in my life and feel like this will be the hardest for me to kick. --Julie

This was a big part of my addiction. It started as part of my ritualization. I was first exposed to pornography as a kid when I woke up and my parents were watching it. My mother did not like it and was saying "what if the kid woke up." That was at age 11. Then at 12 my brother and I found someone's stash in a ditch. We hid in the bushes and looked at it all and shared it with all our friends. I remember being afraid we would be caught, but it was so exciting. My boyfriend in high school had a subscription to "Playboy," "Hustler," and others and we regularly looked at these which seemed to heighten my sexual response. I felt good because I could respond better with porn. Needless to say, I had collected quite a stash of videos, books, magazines, toys, etc. I used all of this during my addiction to avoid intimacy and relationships. Finally the price I was paying wasn't worth it anymore. Price of relationships, cash flow, self esteem, shame - I knew something had to give. Destroying everything plus having someone (or group) you trust holding you accountable, and realizing I wasn't alone, was helpful. I had to make up my mind - and set a date -- to be accountable. --Heidi

Pornography was a great part of how I masturbated and acted out with other men. It started during childhood. My father used it as a way to get him sexually aroused, and it became a way I eventually got sexually aroused. --Ivette

Pornography became a part of my life when I found my first "Playboy" magazine. It inspired me to write stories. Not articles like "Playboy" writes. My mind took off in the direction of the two men who sexually abused me for years. I thought of myself as nice and how they should have treated me and not abused me.

At age 39 I got a computer and started out in chat rooms almost immediately trading pictures and stories of my fantasies. A picture says a thousand words, and I used them to tease and tempt. I used the pictures they sent me to masturbate with. I started with pictures of men. I also liked to look at pictures of women. My addiction progressed and I did not care what the pictures were as long as they were sexual. I had pictures taken of myself to share also on the internet. I used them to lure and meet men, women, and/or couples. I was lost in the fantasy world and the pictures were my new landscape. I tried to stop. I trashed all my pictures after my husband found some. I started again. This time I saved them to disk and hid them (my stash.) I sent my kids to their room so I could have privacy to look at them. I refused social outings, sending the family without me so I could stay home and "look." I lost touch with friends and family during these 2 years (age 39-41). I lost the intimacy with my family, and I lost touch with a lot of reality. Amazingly I kept my job, which I was so proud of. I was holding it together and making it all work. I thought. I did not see until it was too late that I was only going to have my job and nothing else. It took a rude awakening of having my life threatened that made me look at my life. I eased back again. Thought I had control and now no one was being hurt. I was being hurt. In recovery I saw it. While using porn to get my fantasy and "fix" I did not see what was happening to me. Porn was a part of the whole picture. It had to go. --Monica

Pornography, as well as adult novels with explicit sexual descriptions, played a major role in my addiction. At age 7, after having an argument with my mother, I hid in the garage to pretend I had run away. I got really bored, so I started "snooping" around. That afternoon, I found a box of pornography that would change my thought life forever. I also immersed myself in adult novels. At age 10, I read a book that consisted of interviews with women about their sexuality and homosexuality. It intrigued me so much; I read it many times. This literature and the images from the magazines gave me the ability to sexually fantasize for years before I ever had sex. As an adult, my struggle with pornography was mainly of women. Looking at men in pornography never did anything for me. In fact, the few times I went to men's strip clubs, I was bored. I only looked at pornography or watched porn when I was alone. Since I never struggle with masturbation, after engaging in pornography I would act out with men. Today I am extremely fearful of pornography. It is a huge trigger for me. That same fear gives me the ability to run from it. --Tina

This is the part that made it glaringly obvious to me that I had a problem. I started out just looking for toys for my husband and I. Before I knew it, I was planning to meet a guy I had never seen before and swapping pictures back and forth of things that turned us on. I went from pictures of scantily-clad women (which really didn't do anything for me to begin with) to progressively harder stuff - true hard-core - in no time!

My limits were scant. If I had met that guy in the middle of that "zoned out" state, I would have tried it all...and felt terrible afterwards. After awhile this stuff was like oxygen to me. I couldn't move around the house without plopping down at the computer to look up some more pictures. I knew it was affecting every area of my life. I even went out one day with a top on and my pajama bottoms! I was so zoned that I would forget to do normal everyday things. I would wait till the last minute to go pick up my kids or take them to their activities, then I would find myself making all kinds of excuses for it. I was always late. --Rhonda

Porn has been the cornerstone of my addiction ever ince I remember. I was first exposed to it when I was about 5 or so — just "Playboy" and "Joy of Sex." I always looked at women. I never thought I was gay. Porn progressed to the point where I was stealing it at a very young age from my grandfather, neighbors, etc. I flaunted the fact I used porn for masturbation. I thought it was a "cool" way to attract guys (and it did). The content of porn was progressive, meaning, "regular" porn just didn't do anything for me anymore after about age 18. I progressed into much harder core stuff — and eventually got into some pretty deviant stuff. Nothing illegal, though. My porn got to the point where the hardest core wasn't doing anything for me. I believe this is when I really began to act out real stuff much more often. It seems to coincide with my stress and dissatisfaction with my own life.

I haven't purchased any for over a year now — but I really fight with this. For ultimate recovery (for myself), I do not think any porn is okay for me. It is like being an alcoholic. He/she can't just have a sip of wine. I can't just look at 1 picture — I really never know if

I can stop or not. Porn has cost me my career growth (because of the time spent with it). I also think that porn is not talked about much within women's circles because of the shame or embarrassment of it. I really don't know. I just think it must be more prevalent with women than we all know. I am curious to know just how much. I have a difficult time with this subject because of the lack of discussion surrounding porn and women. --Kittie

I began with porn at age 13. I struggled all the way through high school and much of college with it. It has been a major part of my addiction and the shame of that is what drove me to recovery. I've been fairly sober for almost four years, with brief relapses into watching x-rated or excessive fleshy films. Because I've chosen sexual abstinence in relationships and I've chosen to not have intercourse until marriage, I've always thought (until I realized I was addicted) that porn only hurt me, and I was using it just to comfort me. Now I regret and I pray against these friendly "bedfellows," (porn images and characters) I hate that these have taken the joy and innocence away from what I will one day experience with my husband. I've done nothing with my body, but my "eyes" lost their virginity long ago. --Margaret

I was always curious about sex, looking at "Playboy" as a child, but was never obsessed with it. I also enjoyed erotic reading from about age 12 into adulthood. I find that it takes more and more to reach the desired level of stimulation with age and experience. --Yvonne

The role of pornography for some women sex addicts can be a major source of acting out, although this probably does not represent the majority of them. As one woman in a recovery meeting said "Who needs pornography? I can go to any bar, mall, or grocery store and pick someone up and have the real thing." Other women nodded in agreement to this statement.

In our study of women, the use of porn varied. Forty-six percent stated that they use pornography sometimes. Twenty-nine percent stated that they do not use porn. Twenty-one percent stated that they used porn regularly and 4% stated they used pornography rarely in their sex addiction. The internet has made pornography even more available, now it's even on your cell phone.

The types of pornography that women used appears to transcend our stereotypical Playgirl-type magazines. Our study found that 37.5% preferred heterosexual type pornography, 46% preferred pornography of other women, and only 16.5% preferred all male (Playgirl-type) pornography while in their addiction.

Women sex addicts who use pornography can be just as addicted to that form of acting out as any other sexual behavior. Their stories alone tell us this. A woman trapped in self sex and pornography can have just as much shame and guilt as those who act out with others. She has the same negative effects on her self esteem, spiritual life, and her other relationships. She will have the same process of recovery as she heals from the secret of pornography as the other secrets women will share about in the following chapters.

As you choose a path to recovery I strongly suggest not only a porn blocker for your computer but also your cell phone. The porn blocker stops the images from coming on your screen. The accountability software sends a report to those you might be accountable to so you can be honest. These are both available on our website so you don't have to continue to have a secret at what you might be looking at. You are worth protecting your eyes because seeing activates your addiction to do those things you see. You can be free to not be a sex object to yourself or others.

Secret Sexual Abuse

The secret of sexual abuse is by far the most painful secret for a women addicted to sex. Many women who are sexually addicted have been sexually abused. For some, this is what began their addiction. For others, the pain of this secret is what has fueled their sexual addiction. Read on for their poignant stories of how sexual abuse touched their lives.

I was abused when I was 9 by a neighborhood boy who was I did not know what he was doing to me. We often had games with the neighborhood children which involved taking off our clothes. I didn't know this was something I should not do. Now I consider that incident to have been a rape. I told him to stop (the intercourse) but he said, "I'm almost done." I suspect this may have something to do with my addiction, but I'm not sure why. There was another incident with a neighbor boy years later. Also, my dad fondled my developing breasts as he gave me a talk on the birds and the bees and told me I could get condoms from him if I needed them.
--Abby

I was sexually abused by my father from the time I was one year old. It was all oral, digital masturbation. I grew up feeling dirty and bad about myself. I was abused until age 11, then it stopped for 3 years, starting up again when I was 14-18 years-old. I learned masturbation and fantasy from the abuse. The fantasy was to escape the pain. I remember my teenage years especially affecting me as I felt I led a double-life. One life being an academically high achieving girl with the other being a fantasy world of sex, orgies, etc. I did not date in high school and never had a boyfriend either. I was withdrawn, shy, insecure, unsure of myself. There was a lot of repressed feelings inside of me, manifesting itself in depression and mood swings.

I told my husband about the abuse before our marriage. He also was a sex addict, so we fed off each other. I was married to him when I was 17 years old. During that time there was very seldom a night we did not have sex. Also during that time, he had one affair after another, abandoning me (and my 3 kids) to run off with one of his lovers. At the time he left I was 40 years old. I had never dealt with sexual abuse issues in my life. I have been in and out of therapy since then.

I feel like the abuse contributed to my addiction, but I take responsibility today for the behaviors I learned as a child and carried into adulthood. I still feel a lot of pain about the abuse and still am working through the issues. --Debra

It [the abuse] started when I was 4 by a family member and the next door neighbor's son (16 years old). He used to take me into the woods and take all of my clothes off regularly, making me touch him and put my mouth on him. A family member did the same with me, including an approach from behind. I have worked through the anger and have confronted the family member. I am not able to confront the neighbor. I have been disowned by my father and mother. I have forgiven them, and can love them from afar now. I can and do pray for them regularly. I have integrated the abuse into what made me who I am today and use it, plus my experience, to help others. --Heidi

My sexual abuse started at age 3 or 4, if not earlier. It affected my sexuality in not understanding my body and how I felt about myself. It was manifest in adulthood by seeing my body as a way to make someone happy. My sexual abuse was horrible and had many perpetrators, including my mother. I began to hate my body. --Ivette

My father abused me both sexually and physically up until the age of 16 (can't remember when it started). I have allowed the men in my life to abuse me sexually. (I was just reliving my childhood.) To this day, I am unable to be next to my father (much less in the same room) without feeling very creepy and uncomfortable. My father denies all of the abuse (both sexual and physical) to this day. He says that he has "blocked it all out of his mind"—I am working on the concept of forgiveness — not condoning the behavior (because it really screwed me up), but really, really letting it go, so I can feel some sense of freedom from it. --Kittie

My first experience with sexual abuse started and ended when I was about 5 years old. My parents had close family friends that had kids. One of the girls was about 5 years older than me. If I knew then what I know now I would have known that she had been sexually abused herself by someone. She would touch me and have me touch her when I would stay the night. She also taught me masturbation (digital, water, and vibrator). I felt like something was not right, but didn't feel like I should tell anyone. I really looked up to this girl. My next encounter was at 20 with my biological father (I had only known him since I was 17). I was married and had one child (this is when I feel my sexual acting out really started). I found myself attracted to him and one day he followed suit. We actually had an affair for about 2-3 months, he was married at the time and had already had several affairs with other women. I ended the affair (the only relationship that I had ever initiated the end). I categorize this in the sexual abuse section (so was he) that I feel he should have nipped it in the bud. I wish he would have because I feel like I was still acting and thinking so childishly.

My next and final experience is with my husband. I never thought sexual abuse could occur with someone you are married to, but I feel like it has.

I have had times of crying through sex to please my husband. I have said no and he would do it anyway. I have told him no and had him make me feel so wrong that I had sex anyway. I have always been cautious about rape (the kind where a stranger sneaks up in a dark alley), but have had a hard time accepting that rape can also be by someone you trust. --Julie

The first time I went to a therapist I blurted out the whole sexual abuse experience I had from ages 5 through 12. I sat there and poured my heart out. Once I started I could not stop. It felt so good. He was the first person I told. I was scared, happy, and sad at the same time. It was not a secret anymore. One of my perpetrators was dead and another dying. I was an adult and had so much pain locked up and could not change the past, not any of it. I had to give it up to my Higher Power or it would eat at me and erode my foundation. Sharing in group and with my current partner, I worked through the fear and pain. I had to put the stick down and stop beating myself and move on. Forgive myself and those that abused me. I had accepted that as an active sex addict I am not healthy. Neither were my perpetrators. What makes me any more deserving of forgiveness than them? I have forgiven myself and finally them. It is not my place to dole out judgment. I handed it over to a power greater than myself, God. --Monica

I was raised in an emotionally repressive and religiously, rigid family, and have always had issues about being adopted by this family. There were concerns brought up from time to time about my "inheritance" and negative explanations.

Before I had a chance to decide what kind of person I was going to be, I was gang-raped behind my high school by 9 freshman (age 14) I never told my parents. This sparked a rebellion (Phase I) which featured promiscuity and heavy recreational drug use; a phase which ended my first marriage, at age 19. When opportunity came for sex, it did not seem to matter whether I had sex or not, after being raped and degraded by several males. As I became involved in an on-going abusive and degrading relationship with one of those males, that "it doesn't make a difference now" feeling was reinforced. The relationship only ended when he went to jail.

Phase 2 occurred when the first marriage ended in divorce – while divorced I was again driven into promiscuity aided by alcohol, a phase which ended with my second marriage. Most of the 18 years of this marriage, there was no reoccurrence of my being driven into my addiction. This was an abusive relationship which developed, apparently accidentally, when I started to date after my separation/divorce, [which] triggered the "drive" to engage in casual, unprotected, anonymous sex. --Nancy

I was physically/sexually abused as a three-year old child in a day care setting. Later, I was sexually abused by someone I thought was a friend which later turned into a violent, abusive relationship. I first began dealing with the childhood abuse in therapy. About 3 months into my recovery, I was sexually abused by this friend, who knew about my past and was also a survivor. My abuse has profoundly impacted my addiction, most of the porn I viewed, the acting out mistakes I made and even the struggle with masturbation stem out of abuse. I found myself specifically picking porn where females were degraded and/or abused, or punished. I would fantasize about being hurt or abused and often my masturbation would have a "punishing me" aspect to it. Today I would encourage females, who have sexual abuse as a part of their addiction, to not excuse their addiction behind their abuse. They should not neglect their past, as not playing a pivotal role in their addictive behavior, because it DOES! --Margaret

My sexual abuse started when I was 9 or 10 years old. My brother began touching and looking at me. Then he began with the rubbing and taking the clothes off. At first I was very scared but as time passed, I began enjoying it and I think this lead me to pursue it later as something of pleasure. I became very angry with my mother for never knowing about this. I never told her because I feared my brother, and figured I'd be blamed for it all. Since she had no knowledge of this action, she could not be responsible.

At age 17, I was raped by an older guy. I figured it was my fault again. As I have studied and learned about my own addiction, I feel these experiences had a lot to do with my acting out. I still seek to please men as I did to please my brother. I still keep my acting out a secret as I did from my mother. Yes, I feel these abusive situations crippled me sexually, but overcoming them is my choice. How they affect me today is also my choice.--Wendy

As you can see, sexual abuse can be a major influence in both the development and prolonging of sexual addiction. A woman addicted to sex often has a secret about sexual abuse from her past. These painful shadows play a role in her sexual addiction.

Some sexual abuse survivors deal with the pain of the abuse by acting out sexually. This is a way of "medicating" or not dealing with the pain of the sexual abuse as a child, or the rapes as an adult.

Other sexual abuse survivors may feel worthless, "like damaged goods," and that "it doesn't matter anymore." So they totally disregard and abandon themselves into reckless sexual acting out behavior. Another way that sexual abuse can play a major role in their sexual addiction is because of what clinicians call "trauma bonding." In a trauma bond, the female sex addict has actually attached herself to the trauma that she had experienced in childhood. In this case she will tend to repeat the exact same behavior where she is the victim in the situation.

For example, Laurie, a 12 year old girl, was forced to give oral sex to older boys in the neighborhood. This happened to her repeatedly throughout her adolescence. In a trauma bond scenario, this 12 year old girl, now in adulthood, would perform oral sex as her sexual acting out preference. Sexual abuse can be a great influence as to the particular type of sexual behavior, or the environment in which the woman prefers to sexually act out.

In our study we asked several questions about sexual abuse. The following are the results of our study pertaining to sexual abuse.

My first sexual encounter was:

48%   forced physically.
20%   pressured emotionally.
4%   manipulated by threat of abandonment.
28%   chosen freely.

My first sexual encounter was:

44%   sexual abuse.*
12%   rape.*
12%   oral rape.*
12%   positive experience.
20%   none of the above.

*A total of 68% of first encounters being sexual abuse or rape.

My first sexual experience was with:

 4%   a male younger then myself.
30%   a male of the same age.
30%   a male of the same age.
 8%   a male 3-5 years older than myself.*
19%   a male 6-10 years older than myself.*
12%   a male 11+ years older than myself.*
15%   a male adult.*
 0%   a female younger than myself.
 0%   a female the same age as myself.
 8%   a female 3-5 years older than myself.*
 0%   a female 6-10 years older than myself.
 0%   a female 11+ years older than myself.
 4%   a female adult.*

*A total of 54% with age-inappropriate males and 12% with age-inappropriate females.

I believe I was sexually abused:

31%   before age six.
14%   between ages 6-11.
14%   between ages 12-15.
11%   between ages 16-18.
16%   as an adult.
14%   doesn't apply to me

My sexual perpetrators have been:

13%   family members only.
20%   outside of the family.
67%   both family and non-family members.

I have been raped.

65%   Yes
35%   No

Note: Almost 2 out of 3 female sex addicts have been raped.

I have been raped:

47%   1 time.
18%   2 times.
12%   3 times.
23%   4 or more times.

I have been raped by:

41%   1 person.
29%   2 people.
12%   3 people.
18%   Gang raped by 2 or more people.

I believe that my first sexual encounter has had a direct impact on my sexual addictive behavior:

96%   Yes
 4%   No

Note: The percentage that did not feel it was rape or abuse felt their first experience did impact their sexual addiction behavior.

In my addiction I feel I have reenacted my sexual trauma repeatedly.

52%   Yes
18%   No
30%   Does not apply

Reviewing these percentages you can clearly see that the secret of sexual abuse is largely evident in the lives of female sex addicts. A tragic percentage of these women report that they have been sexually abused. This may help to realize that past trauma has a significant role in creating and/or maintaining the sexual addiction. Rape is also a sexual trauma. Sixty-five percent of women who are sexual addicts have reported also being raped. This tragedy causes sexual, emotional, and spiritual pain. The secret of being raped causes much pain for the woman addicted to sex. She often takes false responsibility for the crime such as "If I would not have been drunk...," or "If I would not have dressed and acted that way it never would have happened." This is justification of a rape and rape is always a crime. Secrecy of this abuse can be compounded if the rape occurred while being unfaithful to a husband or partner. Who can she tell without being found out? The need to treat the sexual trauma early in recovery is very important. (I believe this issue is so important that I have devoted an entire video therapy tape alone on this specific issue. This practical video will help to identify what to do to begin to heal from this trauma.)

As you may now realize, many female sex addicts share the secret of sexual abuse. Others in support groups will often be understanding about this secret. The sooner it is shared with someone else, the sooner recovery can begin.

Secret Cycles

Continuing in our study of women sex addicts we asked what the cycle was that drew them into their addiction. Here they will share feelings, thoughts and behaviors that they felt led them into their addictive behavior.

Feelings in My Cycle

1. None - I would NUMB myself, emotionally.
2. Excitement - I would want some kind of excitement.
3. Numb - I would go into a trance state.
4. Intrigue - I would go into the "Hunt."
5. Alive - I would send out signals that I am available (with looks, body movement).
6. Curious - I would single out someone who I felt a strong sexual signal from.
7. Excitement - Attraction to who signalled me back.
8. Comfortable - I would get alone with him.
9. Passion - I would act out sexually.
10. Sadness - I would withdraw emotionally.
11. Numb - I would blot out memories.

--Constance

First I would find some sexual passage in a book perhaps on a TV program. Secondly, I would feel myself beginning to get that high, that excitement. Then I would replay the scene in my mind over and over again while masturbating. --Deborah

First I would find some free time and begin planning excuses to get out. I would then start down my list of po tential partners till I found one available at the time I was. I would lie to my spouse and family and go out to meet a partner. I'd have sex with him and sometimes talk a few minutes. Then return home as if nothing happened. --Wendy

It begins with thoughts, very sexual intense thoughts. Masturbation would begin and then on to meeting men in bars or on the net. I would meet them first, then within the next week have sex. The sex felt great, I felt good, and all of this without any kind of relationship which was great in itself. This cycle is continued with masturbation with a vibrator the day of the anticipated encounter. It felt okay and good until things went out of control when alcohol was factored in. Then I began thinking about the next episode. Sex made me feel good. It's Okay. Alcohol assured me I was okay. If there were feelings of confusion, sex/alcohol was the cure. --Francine

First I would feel lonely, sad, or hurt, and have an obtrusive sexual thought. Or something would remind me of a penis...then my mind would massage the thought. Fantasize. Everything around me would have sexual connotations. Then I would get myself turned on even more about thinking about what I want to do. If possible, I would next watch pornography. I will act out by masturbating wherever I am. I acted out with myself by lighting candles, putting music on. Then I would turn off the lights...Then I would listen to the music and dance to the music as I took off my clothes. Then I would be sexual with myself. --Heidi

First I would see a movie about falling in love with that perfect someone. Then I would get the idea that it should happen to me, and I could make it happen. When I was out and about, someone would catch my eye. Or I would be around someone that would possess a quality I found enticing and I would flirt. That person would either follow suit or not. I could fantasize about that person for a while, at least until I saw him again. If that person could be manipulated, I was the person who could do it. I think a lot of times they were also attracted to me anyway. Next, I would put myself into the right place at the right time. I can't say I had sex with everyone I pursued, but I had at least an emotional affair with them. I felt like all I needed was to make me a person worth knowing. Then I would start feeling bad and not so attracted to that person, and was on to the next person without ever really closing the first. --Julie

First I would light candles, take a hot bath, shave my legs. Then I would drive at least 30 minutes to meet my prey. Then I would put music on, dance for the prey and seduce him. I would take pride in my hunt, capturing the prey. I would perform like I was the best they'd ever had. Only to realize that I was giving my heart, soul, and mind to someone who could care less about me or how good I was at sex. It was just like eating another piece of pizza. Sometimes pizza (sex) has more flavor or toppings on it, but it is still pizza (sex) and it would always satisfy the hunger or craving for pizza (sex). Crazy, but a real analogy. --Laura

First I would make a contact on the internet. Then I would set a time to meet. Sometimes we would go to a mall and talk, or go to dinner. Other times we would go directly to a motel. About half the time we would make arrangements to meet again. --Monica

First I would think about it. Then I would try not to think about it. Next, I would go near places where drinking and meeting men could happen (i.e., bars). I would go in the bars and quietly have a drink or two, get sociable, become a bit friendly, have more to drink...(shyness requires assistance). Then I would disengage usually with a feeling of panic or disorientation. After that, I would start for home, remorse flooded in, and I fought off emotions. I would then turn into steel, pretending normality at home, church, and work. --Nancy

The cycle of my addiction left me with no hope. I had been raped, hurt, and saw myself at the very bottom.--Ivette

First I would feel shame and arousal (either mentally or inspired by external media books, porn, etc.). Then I would shame myself with the pain of the past, either my abuse or the mistakes I'd made with pornography. Next I would masturbate, even 2 or 3 times in one setting, for arousal, for pain/punishment and just because. Then I would usually curl up and cry, or damn myself, or weep brokenly and start again. --Margaret

First I would feel a desire to have sex. If alone, I would usually go to the bedroom, lie on the bed, sometimes even fully clothed, and masturbate. I would almost always fantasize. Then if I saw a man that was my type, and he appeared interested, I would also show interest, by smiling, looking, etc. That was usually enough. If we both knew what we wanted, we would go for it. Many, many times we were outside or in semi public places. I almost never achieved a climax and would later masturbate while replaying or embellishing on the incident. Having sex would always increase my masturbation. --Yvonne

As the above stories demonstrate, women addicted to sex have secret cycles. They may vary from person to person but the cycles they are usually identifiable. Some cycles start with the choosing of their clothes for the day. It is important to identify the cycle so the woman can be alerted or cautious when the red flags of the cycle begin to appear. We will discuss these cycle of addiction now in more detail.

The Addiction Cycle

The addiction cycle pictured on the next page describes the four broad aspects of Pain Agents which are Emotional Discomfort, Unresolved Conflict, Stress, and A Need To Connect. One can discover which of the four main Pain Agents relate. More than one may apply. These Pain Agents and possibly others can move the female sex addict into the next level of the addiction cycle.

I. Pain Agents

In my experience while working with sexual addicts, I have noticed that there is a need to escape and to not feel the pain that they have experienced in the past. Many sex addicts have developed a coping mechanism to escape the pain from childhood and/or an adolescent trauma. This coping mechanism for escape has carried her through most of her adult life. When things get difficult, she will do something to medicate the pain by taking an "emotional aspirin" (act out) to avoid dealing with the trauma from the past.

There are many Pain Agents, four of which we will discuss here, that further the addict into the beginning of the sexual addiction cycle. The beginning of this cycle often starts with a shameful experience. In recovery, when she begins to understand this cycle and is able to identify the red flags, she will be able to short-circuit the necessity to act out by stopping the behavior before it enters the next level of the cycle where it is often more difficult to stop.

The Addiction Cycle

I. Pain Agents
    A. Emotional Discomfort
    B. Unresolved Conflict
    C. Stress
    D. A Need To Connect

II. Disassociation
III. The Altered State
IV. Pursuing Behavior
V. Behavior
VI. Time

A. Emotional Discomfort

Emotional discomfort is one of the primary Pain Agents that will move the addict to the first level of the addiction cycle and cause her to disconnect from her feelings. Emotional discomfort is basically a family-of-origin issue. The sex addict never learned how to identify feelings while growing up in her family. Consequently, many women who are addicted to sex have very primitive emotional skills. Therefore, when she has a painful feeling, she acts out sexually to feel better. She knows that if she just acted out in some way, the feelings would go away temporarily. The interesting thing about this is, it works..*temporarily*! Emotional discomfort for many sex addicts is the Pain Agent that moves them forward into the next steps of the cycle of addiction.

B. Unresolved Conflict

Some sex addicts have been victims of physical, emotional, or sexual abuse, having unresolved issues about the abuse(s). Some have unresolved conflicts about their sexual identity or goals in life. Any kind of unresolved external or internal conflict can agitate the woman addicted to sex. It is this agitation that is an integral part of this particular Pain Agent. Feelings of low self worth can trigger the addict into the addiction cycle. These unresolved conflicts agitate her which is the beginning process for the cycle of addiction.

An example of a trigger point for this Unresolved Conflict might be growing up in a physically abusive home and having unresolved issues around the abuse. When the addict has unresolved conflict, she acts out as a way to avoid, minimize, or medicate this conflict. This can show up in her personal or professional life. For example, the addict may have an argument or misunderstanding with someone at the office or with her husband, and act out as a way to make herself feel better due to this unresolved conflict.

C. Stress

Something we cannot avoid is stress. All of us have stress at some point in our lives. The way a woman addicted to sex medicates, or avoids stress, is by acting out. After acting out, the stress seems to dissipate. However, the fact that the sex addict acted out creates more stress which makes a cycle for her to keep adding stress to the Pain Agent, and recreate the cycle. Many women addicted to sex set up these dynamics in which they repeat this behavior by creating stress so that they can alleviate the stress by acting out.

Stress can be located in several areas in the addict's life. It can come from the realm of her family or vocation. It can be from the pressure of finances, as many sex addicts have difficulty budgeting money. Stressors can be tied to close relationships or to the family of origin. It can be about spiritual issues. Just the everyday grind of driving through traffic can be stressful for some. Stress -- pressure from outside -- can move her into a Pain Agent and back into the cycle of addiction.

D. A Need to Connect

Every human being has a need to connect. I believe that everyone is born with a need to touch and be touched. Many women who are sexual addicts act out sexually as a primary way of being satiated inside. It is through this Altered State and false nurturing that the addict feels like she is connected. This can be very confusing for her in recovery since in the past it has been a way to connect with her sexual addiction. This need to connect can move her further into the Addiction Cycle, if she doesn't find other healthier ways to meeting this need to connect. I have found that when female sexual addicts feel this need to connect, they also feel pain because they don't know how to get this relational need met. She is faced with the pressure to act out in order to make the pain of being unable to connect go away.

II. Disassociation

A common clinical term used in the treatment of addictions and traumas is disassociation. Disassociation simply means that the woman addicted to sex disconnects from herself. Many addicts disconnect while driving. They may find that they have drifted off into all kinds of thoughts and pictures, and sometimes it may be difficult to concentrate. Often the woman addicted to sex works at jobs much lower than her skill level because she disassociates so frequently. She may even choose not to work at all so she can be free to act out as she chooses. Disconnecting is a way that many sexual abuse victims survive from the pain of their past. These victims most likely disconnected during their trauma as well. Disconnecting while growing up in a dysfunctional home may have been a survival tool when the environment was not supportive.

Disassociating or disconnecting is the very beginning of the cycle and yet is still a separate stage of the cycle of addiction itself. Disassociation is necessary for the addiction cycle to take place. It can be compared to an airplane traveling down the runway. There is a distinct time that it is on the ground and another distinct time when it has lifted off the runway and is disassociated. Disassociation is important to understand because it is at this time that we can use behavioral techniques to get grounded. Getting grounded can be as simple as making a phone call or going to a support group. It is while the addict is disassociated, and not far along yet in the addiction cycle, that she may still have enough sanity left to keep the plane on the ground before it takes off to the next level of the addiction cycle. This is crucial for the woman addicted to sex to understand, so that she can be aware when she is checking out and is not totally available.

Disassociation is the stage after the feelings of past or present pain have been felt. The addict needs to do something with her pain and so she disassociates. Then she enters into the beginning of the cycle of addiction.

III. The Altered State (Fantasy World)

Another clinical term we use for trauma survivors and addicts is the Altered State. Moving into this state is what the recovery community often calls "the bubble." The bubble is a place the addict may have created during her childhood or adolescence that she identifies as a safe place. Some even have names for the place they go to, although for most the Altered State is simply a place to "check out" or fantasize. It is a place where the addict creates images or behaviors that may be sexual in nature.

The Altered State can be very appealing and soothing. Many women that I have counseled identify this as the time they go on the hunt for a victim. This Altered State is also when she is deciding what clothes to wear or during her bathing rituals. For some, it is the moment they enter into a bar, club or, social place they frequent for victims. It is an emotional oasis that the women may have created thousands of times. It can include pornography or fantasy about other people, even though she may not actually have had any affairs. We can describe it as the imaginary place the sex addict goes to, as she looks at others while she walks in the mall. Just as a computer scans a picture into its file, she may take the picture of the person she scanned and place it in her computer file in her mind to use later to fantasize during her Altered State.

The Altered State is where the addict goes to when she closes her eyes. It is similar to the analogy of the plane. The addict has her Pain Agent, the plane is on the ground, then she decides it is too painful to handle her thoughts on her own. So the plane takes off and begins a climb to a cruising altitude. The woman goes into the Altered State when she reaches the cruising altitude and the plane levels off. She is now in a different reality. In this altered reality, she is in total control. She can control every image and person in this Altered State. She can control other individuals' speech and behavior, no matter how degrading or nurturing it may be. She can create unlimited possibilities. In this fantasy world of an Altered State, she is all-powerful, all-knowing, in control, loved, cared for, and significant. The Altered State, or nirvana, is where she has disconnected and checked out. This is a very important part of the sexual addiction cycle. Once she has entered the Altered State, if she doesn't make a phone call soon to someone she can be accountable to, or pierce "the bubble" somehow by getting back into reality, she will probably move into the next level of the Cycle of Addiction which is the pursuing the behavior.

IV. Pursuing Behavior

Once the addict has achieved the level of the Altered State that she created in the bubble, or the Altered State, she will now head toward a destination. She may have sophisticated or unsophisticated ways of doing this. Nonetheless, a behavior will be pursued. The pursuit of this this behavior can be very complicated. The woman addicted to sex has specific repetitious behaviors and once she enters the Altered State, she is going to pursue a behavior and act out in some way. It may be pursued alone, with others or in fantasy. The female sex addict is on the lure, hunt, or pursuit, much like a plane going to its destination. She has gone from reality to fantasy, and now she is going to create whatever her Altered State wants. She is trying to satiate something that is insatiable, and she has experienced this many times.

During the pursuit, some women have specific places they go, people they see, phone calls they make, but whatever it is, they are in pursuit of a repetitious behavior. For some it may be a very clearly identified location. Some addicts have described it like this, "Yes, I was on my way to a particular place, and was totally out of control. I couldn't feel myself touching the ground at all." At this point, the female sex addict has experienced all the physiological symptoms of being in the Altered State and has pursued the behavior.

Pursuing the behavior is a very difficult stage to break, unless you have the support of someone who can help you somehow pierce the bubble and get you back into reality.

V. Behavior

The behavior of a woman addicted to sex can range from being sexual with themselves, exhibitionism, pornography, or being sexual with others, and can include criminal behaviors. The behavior of each woman is different, but the experience is the same. Once the sexual addict goes through the stage where she pursues a behavior; she continues by acting out sexually. The addict connects her sexuality to whatever her Altered State is pursuing at the time, and repeats this behavior over and over again. Every time that she goes through this cycle and acts out, she reinforces neurologically and psychologically that this behavior is going to medicate her inner being. The reinforcement of this repetitive behavior is her way of dealing with pain and stressors.

This final behavior completes the cycle of addiction. This is where she "acts out" as they say in Twelve Step groups. This sexual release combined with the Altered State reinforces her sexual addiction. Those who are in support groups, and continue to act out in one way or another, won't get better, and their lives won't change if they continue to act out sexually in any way within this cycle. They will basically continue to stay addicts. The best and only way they can "stay clean" is if they don't reinforce the sexual addiction cycle. This "acting out" behavior completes the cycle of addiction except for one other item -- time.

VI. Time

I have counseled many sex addicts from various cultural and socioeconomic backgrounds, and there appears to be an individual pattern for each person. But each person has a definite pattern -- and knowing their pattern is the key to recovery.

Some women who are sexual addicts have sexual acting-out binges. Others' acting-out behaviors are much further apart. For most though, there seems to be a set time for the recurrence of pain and the actual acting out behavior. The time between one act and another may be hours, days, weeks, or months. There is time between one Pain Agent and another Pain Agent. Between these times, if the addict can incorporate her support groups, phone calls, and recovery, she can strengthen herself so that when the next Pain Agent comes, she can cope with it -- rather than giving herself permission to act out because of the pain.

Time is a tricky issue. But between behaviors is her best opportunity to cope before the cycle starts. Pain comes into everyone's life, and that can not be controlled. But what can be controlled is what can be done with one's time. So when the emotional discomfort, unresolved conflict, or need to connect comes along, one can have the strength to say "no" to the addiction, by doing something healthy with it instead.

As an addict, there is a need to feel the pain and stay in reality. Finding positive behaviors to reinforce that one has value and is worth recovery is imperative. The sex addict and her family is worth recovery so that they can live a full life physically, emotionally, and spiritually. Time can become a best friend. The longer between the last acting-out behavior, at any level, the better life can become. Without support, time can be the only thing that keeps her from her next acting out experience. I would encourage the woman to memorize her patterns of pain, disconnecting, altered state, and pursuing behavior so that she can begin a successful journey toward recovery.

Secret Addict

In the field of addiction there is a helpful tool of personifying the addiction. This tool goes back to Alcoholics Anonymous support group meetings in the 1930s where one alcoholic would say to another "My alcoholic was really taking me for a ride today." Putting the addiction into a personification has helped many addicts (of any type) gain insight into their addiction and facilitate honesty about themselves during recovery. In the various sexual addiction Twelve Step support group meetings the personification of the sexual addiction being called "my addict" is quite common among the members. Below are the writings of ten women in various stages of recovery from sex addiction discussing their personified "addict" and how it "talks" to each one of them.

She is smart. She knows what she wants and that is sex only. No relationships or the like. She goes out on a mission to obtain this through the internet or in bars. She can attract men easily. She must have a special look as men will approach her without any flirting on her part, and this is a mystery to her. It can happen anywhere, the grocery store, mall, work, just anywhere. She meets the person, goes to dinner, then within the next week the stage is set for sex. Only at her home. Her script includes "this will feel good," "sex is a high," "sex is not addictive so don't worry about the alcohol addiction," "don't worry about the feelings of the person, get what you want!" She dresses conservatively as this is intriguing and she is, after all, a professional legitimate working person during the day. The men must know that. --Francine

I find my addict to be a liar. She would say anything and everything to not be caught, although she did many things to get herself caught. She can manipulate a person and make them feel confused, then go in for the kill. I feel like she is a sad person who desires atten-tion. Lonely and depressed, she goes out to hunt for people to pull into her web. I think she really wants to be liked, she just thinks no one will like her as she is. I think she fears aloneness. She will use other people's care-giving instinct to lure them in by telling needy stories. She picks men that are "easy" or a "sure thing" so that she will never be rejected. She really likes to read erotic books. She makes me think these behaviors are all right so I will increase my sex drive for my husband. She leads me away from other women friends by centering on men. She knows if I could really be friends with another woman, I could desert her and her controlling ways. I could get my own self-esteem and leave her in the gutter. --Julie

My addict always had to keep busy, never could be alone. She would think and plan all the ways she could meet a man. She was desper-ate. She would tell me that my life was boring and I was just trying to have some fun and excitement. --Debra

My addict had no heart. She used others at their own expense. She was extremely dominant, yet hurt. She planned nothing except her next encounter. She thinks she is dirty and not worth anything. --Ivette

She is very sneaky. Her words are very sweet and sexy. She is very aggressive, and even if told no by a man the first time, she pursues until she scores with him. She uses the fact that her husband is not very active as an excuse. Playing on men's sympathies. Making them feel needed and wanted. She begins planning a time alone with them. When they get together it is very clear what the purpose is. After she leaves, she then begins fantasizing about it being a lov-ing relationship. That "he" actually cares. I usually end up feeling guilty and hurt because of the thoughts of an actual relationship that never happens. --Wendy

She can cheat me out of my religious convictions. When I am horny, sex is all that matters. If there is a man handy, I'll use him for some extra pleasure. My addict even talks me into thinking it is okay to take advantage of a minor. She makes me believe that if he says he will not report me to the police, he won't. She makes me believe I won't get any sexually transmitted diseases, that the condom won't break, or I won't get pregnant. She will do absolutely anything to convince me that orgasm is everything.

I am a very responsible person, for the most part, but my addict can talk me into doing the most absurd, non-religious, irresponsible things one can imagine. Then, when she is satisfied with an orgasm, she abandons me to my more coherent thinking. Feelings that come when she leaves me in the lurch include despair, regret disbelief at what I've done, shame, and remorse for hurting the person involved.

When she's gone, I no longer want to touch a man. Wild horses can't drag me back into bed with him. Sometimes I see I am abusing him. I am like a black widow who uses him and discards him. Sucks the life out of him. Intimacy is not in the picture. Sex, raw pleasure, is all that matters. I don't matter, he doesn't matter, and nobody else does, either--including God. --Abby

My addict is cunning and convincing...anything that will build her ego up. She is looking for praise outside of herself. She thinks men need to be attracted to her to be worth-while or valuable. She avoids pain or strong emotions. She numbs out. Once she decides she wants a man she will do anything to get him. Once she gets an obsession in her mind she starts making plans. She would go to the bar and scope out the men sending sexual signals, waiting to receive the right one back. After she connects with someone she carries the act out. Each time taking a little more of herself away until there is nothing left but emptiness and pain, and bewilderment as to how she got there. She thinks she is powerful because she can attract men. In reality she is powerless.--Constance

I would describe her as rebellious. She loves to flirt, to lust and be lusted after. She likes to be the one in control. She doesn't think much of her self worth, and is filled with rage. In her selfishness, she spends hours preparing, with long baths and a cold beer. A skin care regiment and careful application of makeup is a must. She can spend 30 minutes blow-drying her curly brown hair, silky straight. The outfit was never "cheezy", but tight, sexy, and sophisticated. She would walk through a room and be filled by attention. And the man she was having an illicit affair with would go crazy inside for her. Then as they would sneak off, it would be intense. Afterwards, she could live on the images of the night in her mind for days. The voice in her head told her how beautiful she must be for men to be unfaithful to their girlfriends and wives. She had the ability to keep her actions completely separate from her marriage or committed relationships. She had a lot of practice. And sadly, she had a way of pushing away the people that truly loved her. She was so deep in denial, she never realized that she was dying inside. --Tina

Lots of denial, lots of justifications. I was the queen of justification. I also think my addict has a great ability to compartmentalize my life so as not to have to face my addiction head on. My addict is always with me. Ever so subtly. And at times raging. She uses the lines of "a little bit won't hurt," "you can always stop," "you are sober so it is okay," and, "just this time" or "one last time won't hurt." I used to believe that anything between two consenting adults was okay as long as it didn't hurt anyone else around you. I now know that was my addict alking giving me a big justification for me to do anything I pleased.--Kittie

My addict is sneaky, plots and plans, and is always on the lookout for men, for private places to have sex. She always has a "come on" look. --Yvonne

In these quotes, I believe the different emotions and thoughts they experienced can be felt. Every "addict" is different. Every woman who has the secret of sexual addiction has different wounds, or needs, that the "addict" is trying to medicate. Each woman will take her own journey to disentangle herself from the addict.

The good news is that anyone can grow beyond this secret, and she (the addict) can be less and less a part of their life and heart.

Secret Consequences

In every addiction there are consequences. For the over-eater, it is weight. For the spendaholic, it is debt, and for addictions like alcohol and drugs, it may be family or job problems. Sex addiction is no different as it also has its own array of consequences. The following stories detail the adverse consequences from the lives of women addicted to sex.

Several areas that can suffer consequences due to a life-style of sexual addiction are Marriage, Lovers, Health Issues, Pregnancy and Abortions, Other Addictions, Self-Esteem, Depression, and Parenting. We will discuss each one of these consequences in this chapter along with the stories of women whose lives were unfortunately affected by them.

Marriage

My sex addiction greatly affected my marriage. I was never truly committed to this person. I led a double life in my acting out years. I appeared to be responsible and faithful. We built our lives up, had good jobs and built a house getting ready for a family. Then I had a secret affair. I did not want to be honest that I really wasn't attracted to the other man. I was selfish. I wanted my cake and to eat it too. There had been a pattern of me setting up situations where

I would have two men fighting over me. This fed my ego, giving me false self esteem. The affair was very harmful to all involved. The marriage and the affair was based on dishonesty and selfishness. I left both, only to get with someone else a little later on. My sexual addiction really affected this second marriage shortly thereafter. We divorced. Then I had an affair on my boyfriend with my ex-husband-insanity! --Constance

It destroyed my first marriage. My selfishness and self-centeredness brought constant conflict between my husband and I. I blamed him for my emptiness. I had a beautiful home, filled with great furniture. I drove a sports car and there was never a shortage of savings. None of these things filled the hole in my heart. During the first two years of marriage I remained "outwardly" faithful to my husband. But my thought life was out of control. I couldn't wait to lie down at night and act out in my thoughts. By the third year of marriage, I crossed the line into adultery. --Debra

I always had a feeling of unworthiness and basic dishonesty before self, God, husband, and others. Most recently, relapses have greatly saddened me by the change in sacredness and specialness of marriage, by my infidelity.

I love my husband very much and want to stay with him. I have hurt him deeply by my addiction as he knows I have been with others, and that I am trying to stop, but it seems impossible. We have 4 children who know nothing of my addiction, so far. Three years ago I had an affair with a pastor and it destroyed his ministry, and my husband was fired from his pastoral position from that church. I can never undo the harm that caused either man. I live with that guilt and the effects it had on the congregation. I have withdrawn from my husband. I don't trust telling him anything about my addiction, for fear of who he'll "counsel" with and tell.

We have lost that daily closeness with each other, and the spiritual oneness we once had. We are hanging on to threads right now. I don't know what the straw will be that breaks the camel's back. He has put up with an awful lot and still loves me, someday that love will stop covering his eyes, and he'll see me for what I am. If he leaves me, I will have lost all hope, my rock, and my shelter. I love him but I can't seem to stop my obsession with sex. The other men mean very little to me. I have one I feel very fond of but, not the true meaning of love I have with my husband. This probably makes little to no sense to most people, but I mean it most sincerely. --Wendy

My marriages (especially the 2nd one) began by being based on sex. I slept with the guys first, and then married them. In both of my marriages there was swinging and other stuff involved. I manipulated with sex. I/we avoided confrontation with sex. My first marriage ended because of his alcoholism.

I am still married to the second (10 years now), though we are in the process of divorce. I cheated on every relationship I ever had including my marriages. I was able to justify the cheating. I do believe that my "stinking thinking" really got in the way of my ever having a chance of developing a healthy relationship. I chose emotionally unavailable mates. And I was emotionally unavailable, and needy at the same time as well. When I chose to become healthier and join SLAA [Sex and Love Addicts Anonymous], going through treatment, my marriage was in trouble. I became stronger as a result of the program in my own spiritual growth, but my husband became evidently weaker as he found he could no longer try to control me. He told me that he felt that sex was one of the last bonds that he and I had together and that he was afraid that SLAA was going to take that away from us. As I became more of a present (in mind) person, looking for less escape (less of my drug of choice), he panicked more about our relationship. He went out and had two affairs (he is currently involved in one of them). He is still addicted to Internet stuff, and because he has never chosen his own path of recovery, we have sadly grown very apart. --Kittie

As these stories describe, marriages can be deeply damaged, scarred, and/or destroyed by the effects of a life-style of sexual addiction. The lack of intimacy, honesty, and fidelity are all a part of the acting out and all parties are usually affected by them. In this section discussing marital consequences, our study will disclose statistics on the marital status, multiple marriages, and the number of affairs in each marriage.

The following is the marital status identifying the women who co-operated in our study.

56%   Married,
22%   Divorced, and
22%   Single (never married).

The number of times married:

39%   1 time
39%   2 times
0%   3 times
22%   4 or more times

In my first marriage I have had:

21%   no affairs.
26%   1-2 affairs.
21%   3 affairs.
16%   4-10 affairs.
0%   11-20 affairs.
11%   21-30 affairs.
5%   more than 31 affairs.

Note: Average length of marriages was 10 years.

In my 2nd marriage I have had:

45%   no affairs.
11%   1-2 affairs.
11%   3 affairs.
33%   4-10 affairs.

Note: Affairs are less frequent in 2nd marriage.

The women responding to our study were asked if they had lost their marriage due to their sexual addiction. The following were the results.

45%   Yes, I have lost a marriage.
55%   No, I have not lost a marriage.

Lovers

Women addicted to sex may go outside of a committed relationship sexually. However, this may have started in her dating pattern prior to marriage. In our study, we asked how monogamous these women were in their dating relationships:

In dating relationships I have been:

4%   totally monogamous.
48%   mostly monogamous.
48%   not monogamous.

As we know, dating sometimes turns into marriage and marriage doesn't necessarily mean change for sex addicts. In our study we asked several questions about lovers outside of the marriage, or committed relationship.

Are these men that women sex addicts are acting out with, outside of their marriage, one night stands or are long-term affairs? How long do these relationships or encounters last? The answers to these questions vary from addict to addict. Some women addicted to sex never are unfaithful in marriage, but act out only with themselves.

The women who act outside of their marriage vary in what they are looking for in this extramarital sexual relationship. Some women want to act out with someone they don't know or even care about. Another may only want men of power (money, position, or friend of husband). Still others want to have a few "regular" fixes. These fixes are usually men who will act out with them almost anytime they call. If this isn't confusing enough, some will go through stages of acting out one way and then switch to a different victim profile and some "do it all" with no boundaries. The following are stories with various victim profiles.

The first experience was with a co-worker. I had fantasized about him and flirted with him for about two years. My second experience was soon after, when I met a man at my favorite out of town resort. I acted out with him every time I visited the area. The third was the most risky. My husband's best friend lived across the street from us. After flirting with him for a good 6 months, the opportunity came up one night when both our spouses were gone for the weekend. We engaged in our affair for about 4 months. We used to meet in the wee hours of the morning in his garage while our spouses were sleeping. It had to be so obvious as we interacted at social gatherings. During the same time, I started an affair with a man who worked out at the same gym. This continued about 6 months. Before it ended I met another man and engaged with him for almost two years. I always pretended that "they were the only one" each man did not know about the other. Both my husband and I were in complete denial. He had to have known. Three years later and after a series of events the greatest event being my surrender to God, I told my husband about the affairs. He admitted his suspicions but never wanted to face the truth. He said that if I was willing to stop this behavior he was willing to start all over and work on the marriage. I was shocked. I was also completely inadequate to do so. I could not imagine myself not being able to get my "fix" on illicit sex again. How could I function without it? Broken and in complete despair, I let him walk away.--Debra

I acted out both with people I knew, as well as those I didn't. It didn't matter to me. Both conquests were highs for me. I have been with my husband's friends, their girlfriends, my roommates, coworkers, prostitutes, dancers, swingers, and other various people. I think I have been with somewhere around 20-30 women and somewhere around 60-70 men. Some of my more recent acting out (year ago and more) was with my affair.--Kittie

All about the addict/narcissist/emotional manipulator's needs + desires, trying to fill a huge, deep void.

The people I acted out with were sexually attractive to me, some I knew from work, some were total strangers. I would usually look for someone that was unusual in some way, or not the norm -- like a different race or someone from different social structure to make it more exciting. I felt intrigue and excitement. I felt I was special to be able to attract these people. I also felt a sense of power that I could conquer these people. Now I just feel sad and embarrassed that I would treat people like a trophy. I feel sad for the addict who felt she needed to conquer people to feel good about herself.--Constance

People I have acted out with...well 4 of them were from work...police officers and politicians. One was an old boyfriend and one was a new acquaintance who is as lonely as I am. The men from work I liked because of their power. I used it to my benefit. They were very confident and I liked that. Now I just feel like a toy on the shelf for them that they call upon when they want sex. The old boyfriend was a one-time deal. So I felt that was a mistake. The new acquaintance is scared of an emotional relationship and is going nowhere, so I feel I used him.--Wendy

I could pretty much act out with anyone. Everyone had some kind of appeal to me that I could expound on. One guy I acted out with many times. I feel like I hate him, but I really don't care one way or the other. One guy I feel guilty about. I think he was healthy; I just hope I didn't warp him. I regret having sex with one guy, who I think was wonderful. Mostly I just feel like I treated those people badly, like I used them. I don't like that at all. I really think of myself as a good person and friend, although I don't really know how to just be friends. I really thought I wanted those people, but what I really wanted was friendship. I just didn't know how to get them to like me or how to make myself special to them except to make them, be infatuated with me.--Julie

" fantasy "

Continuing in our inquiry of encounters outside of the marriage or committed relationship, we asked how many affairs our respondents had and where they found others to act out with. The following are the results of this research.

41%   All affairs
35%   Mostly affairs with some one night stands
18%   Mostly anonymous encounters with some affairs
 6%   All one night stands

The people I had sex with I would initially meet at:

26%   clubs/bars.
10%   mostly at work.
19%   mostly social settings.
19%   mostly friends.
26%   while out and about.

As you can see, the encounters they had and where they found their acting out partner also varies. Some women groom their prey over time, others just meet someone in a club and act out.

In this study we asked if they had a certain profile of persons that they acted out with. Fifty percent said yes, they had a certain victim profile. The other 50% stated that there were no perimeters for the victims they chose.

The length of the relationship the addict would have with a person outside of her committed relationship varied also.

The average length of sexual relationships outside my marriage was:

17%   just one night stands.
28%   2-6 weeks.
44%   6 weeks to 6 months.
11%   many years.

Health Issues

I've experienced the loss of innocence and the ability to see sex as it was intended. I've suffered medical loss because of my acting out and the pain I've created for myself through masturbation. There were also some financial consequences because of my "stash" of porn. I've spent about $300 on materials. I never used checks or cards because I was afraid of being caught. Another consequence was lost time. When I think of all the long, lonely, dark hours alone struggling with this, or the events and things I was late to because I was in my addiction--I've lost whole segments of time!
--Margaret

Sex in our generation definitely has its health issues as a devastating consequence. The number of sexually transmitted diseases seems to grow each decade. Women addicted to sex are exposing themselves to short-term and long-term health issues.

The first question related to Health Issues asked to women sex addicts was about condom usage. The responses reinforce that they take serious health risks and pregnancy risks by not using condoms.

In my addiction I:

0%	always used a condom.
27%	mostly used a condom.
9%	sometimes used a condom.
37%	rarely used a condom.
27%	never used a condom.

What about sexually transmitted diseases? We asked how many sexually transmitted diseases were contracted while they were in the midst of their sexual addiction. The results are probably what you may expect after reading the responses from the previous question.

In my addiction I:

29%   have contracted 1 STD.
14%   have contracted 2 STD's.
 5%   have contracted 3 or more STD's.
52%   have not contracted any STD's.

Note: Almost half of female sex addicts have contracted an STD.

The health conditions that these women contract vary from person to person. The women who did contract health problems also shared what types they contracted. They are:

- Genital Herpes
- Condyloma
- Bacterial Vaginal
- Yeast Infections
- Chlamydia
- Pelvic Inflammatory Disease
- Vaginal Infections
- Venereal Warts
- Bladder Infections
- Gonorrhea

The reality of contracting a sexually transmitted disease is a very genuine possibility for a female sex addict. The reality of this is obvious for others to see after looking at the risks that she often takes. However as with any addict, she rarely thinks through any of the future consequences of what could happen while she is in the midst of her addiction.

In our study, the issue of regular testing for STD's was also addressed. The respondents of our study stated that 30% of them have been tested for STD's, while 20% have never been tested. The women in our study also answered the question as to how often they have been tested for STD's.

I have been tested for STD's:

 4%   quarterly.
13%   2 times a year.
 9%   1 time a year.
48%   less than once a year.

13%   never.
13%   does not apply.

Sexually transmitted diseases are probably the largest health consequence that a female sex addict may experience. Unfortunately STD's are not the only health risk that she may have due to her secret sexual addiction. In this study there was a section for the respondents to answer regarding other medical problems they felt they had experienced due to their sexual addiction. Below is a listing of some of them.

- Depression
- Scarring of cervix
- Migraine Headaches
- Yeast Infections
- Bipolar Disorder
- Alcoholism/Drug Abuse

- Anxiety
- Ulcers
- Fatigue
- Herpes
- Nausea
- Psychiatric Problems

As this list tells us, there are many different medical issues that can be related to the secret of sexual addiction. This addiction can have many health consequences, including one which we have yet to discuss.

Pregnancy and Abortion

My losses: A pregnancy (abortion), my marriage #2, a couple of jobs, career advancement, my sense of self-worth, my pride, my dignity, a very good guy (boyfriend), never graduated college, lost respect from friends, alienated other friends, and possibly the chance to ever have a child of my own (this is the most difficult for me to face). --Kittie

I had pregnancy scares, getting caught, (not actually in the act but when I told the honest truth, the guy lied about it). Never being able to tell the whole, honest, truthful story to anyone. Shame. I was also stalked for many years. --Yvonne

I have listened to many secret stories over the years and these stories vary greatly from person to person, but rarely do the tears flow more readily than when a woman talks about pregnancies and abortions which occurred in the midst of her sexual addiction. The pain of lost children -- some are born and given up for adoption, and some never see the light of day due to an abortion--is tremendous. These women have told me vividly of their abortion experiences and how emotionally painful they were. For some this excruciating experience is a turning point for recovery, and for others multiple abortions and other unfortunate consequences indeed have to occur before the seeking of recovery ever happens.

Pregnancies and abortions are very dark and deep secret consequences for the woman addicted to sex. These secrets alone can leave her heart so full of pain that she continues to medicate herself through her sexual addiction.

The statistics shared on the following page are related to: unplanned pregnancies conceived outside of the marriage or committed relationship, abortions, and the lasting emotional distress resulting from the destructive life-style that sexual addiction brings to any willing partner.

I have been impregnated outside of marriage.

21%   Yes
79%   No

The pregnancies outside of my marriage were:

50%   Aborted
33%   Born
17%   Miscarried

I have been impregnated outside of a marriage or long-committed relationship:

9%   1 time

9%	2 times
4%	3 times
4%	4 times
13%	5 or more times
61%	Does not apply

I have aborted a pregnancy:

17%	1 time
17%	2 times
13%	3 times
4%	4 times
8%	5 or more times
41%	Does not apply

I still have emotional pain about my abortions:

| 85% | Yes |
| 15% | No |

Other Addictions

In the field of addictions, it is not uncommon for multiple addictions to be present. For some women the use of alcohol or drugs may be necessary to lure them to act out sexually. For others, the other addictions are totally separate addictions. In our study we asked the women to answer questions related to other possible addictions including alcohol, drugs, and eating disorders. These questions were asked in the context of their active, sexual acting-out days and some during their recovery as well.

I feel that I have struggled with eating disorders.

| 52% | Yes |
| 48% | No |

The eating disorder I have struggled with is:

66%   Overeating
17%   Anorexia
17%   Bulimia

I have had a problem with alcohol during my addiction.

50%   Yes
50%   No

I have had a problem with alcohol during my recovery from sex addiction.

17%   Yes
83%   No

Note: Recovery significantly impacted alcohol problems.

I have had a problem with illegal drug usage during my sex addiction.

27%   Yes
73%   No

I have had a problem with illegal drugs during my recovery from sex addiction.

 4%   Yes
96%   No

The above responses demonstrate that the issue of alcohol and drugs does seem to get better once she starts recovery from her sexual addiction. If one is struggling with other addictions, it needs to be determined if it is related to the sexual addiction. Often if you treat the primary addiction, the lesser or supporting addiction may go into remission. One way of finding out if it is a supporting addiction (i.e., "I drink so I can act out sexually") is to go into remission with the sex addiction. If alcohol stays and is still causing a problem for the sex addict after recovery, both addictions may have to be addressed simultaneously.

Self-Esteem and Depression

In the course of any addiction, self-esteem and depression can be a core issue. For some the feelings of low value occurred prior to the addiction. In the following story, one woman attempted to get her value through acting out sexually.

In my addiction, my sexual attractiveness was the most important thing--all that my self-esteem was built on. --Veronica

For other women with the secret of sexual addiction it is the addiction that affects the self esteem. Here is what Laura had to say about hitting bottom with her sex addiction and the effects it had on her self esteem.

Extreme exhaustion from trying to make sex turn to love or what I thought was love. Physical pain and swelling of my body from too much sex either by myself, or other indulgences. But finally, it was the self disgust I felt, as well as the horrifying self-esteem that broke the camel's back. I felt so unhappy, unlovable, and disgusting. Pathetic to my family, friends, and self.--Laura

Further questions about self-esteem and depression were asked in our study.

In the active days of my addiction, my self-worth was:

63% very low
29% low
 4% average
 4% high

In recovery from addiction, I feel my self-esteem was:

9%   very low
48%   low
30%   average
13%   high

I feel that I struggle with depression.

83%   Yes
17%   No

The results of the self-esteem questions again give hope of improving self-esteem in recovery. I think it is obvious that the women who chose to recover from their secret addiction additionally improved their self esteem.

My experience as a clinician specializing in sex addiction is that some sex addicts do use sex as a way to treat their depression. One way you can determine if depression is an issue alone and not due to the addiction is to stay sexually sober, including masturbation, for about six weeks. This period of time will separate the mood swings from the feelings of withdrawal from sex addiction. If the feelings of depression are still current then the addict may need to visit a medical doctor for an evaluation.

Parenting

An area that many women pride themselves in is parenting. Any addiction effects primary relationships. Children are a primary relationship.

Sex addiction does impact parenting in various ways. One effect is that it robs the addict of being as emotionally or spiritually mature as they would be without being in an active addiction. A second side effect is the feelings of guilt, shame and betrayal due to the lower priority being given toward the child. The list goes on.

The following are stories exhibiting some of the parental consequences that Wendy, Constance, Julie and Yvonne experienced in the midst of their sexual addiction life-style.

I feel I have not been there for my children as much as I should have been even though I really tried to make them a priority above spouse and work. I have spent time on the internet when my kids needed help with their homework, I have lied about where I had been. I've been late picking them up because I was with someone. I have refused to take them "shopping" when I was really going to meet a partner. I hate all this. Someday they will know of my addiction. It will crush their image of me. If they do not know before they are 21 years old, I plan to tell them so they understand the possible hereditary effects.--Wendy

I believe I've never become a parent due to sexual addiction/anorexia. I had not been able to form a mature close bond with anyone. I had abortions due to my sexual promiscuity.--Constance

I feel like I have been trying to be a good parent while sitting in a glass box. I can see everything that happens to my children, but can't truly get to them. I have a real problem with love and emotions even with my kids. I keep reminding myself that I don't want my kids to grow up unhealthy. I want them to have a parent that is active in their lives. My kids know how to play by themselves while mommy is busy, but I am now teaching (showing) them that I am there for them too. I now play with them and listen to them. I am not wrapped up in myself any more. They are doing wonderfully. --Julie

I feel I was always a good parent, but I still feel it affected the kids. I think they noticed, and I, of course, was always looking [for a man/conquest] which detracted from the quality of time spent with them. --Yvonne

Women who are in recovery from sex addiction state that their parenting has improved greatly. They say things like "I'm definitely more present with my children" and "I actually enjoy the little things now. Where was I before?" Recovery often can help restore this area.

Secret Anorexia

It may appear unusual to read a chapter called intimacy anorexia in a book pertaining to sexual addiction. During our research study, we surveyed female sex addicts, male sex addicts, and the wives of male sex addicts on the problem of sexual/intimacy anorexia. We were surprised to find that when measuring sexual/intimacy anorexia in the lives of sexual addicts, female sex addicts scored higher on sexual anorexia than their male counterparts. Thirty-nine percent of female sex addicts met criteria for sexual/intimacy anorexia. Twenty-nine percent of the male sex addicts also met criteria for sexual/intimacy anorexia.

What is intimacy anorexia? Intimacy anorexia is simply the active withholding of oneself spiritually, emotionally, and sexually from the primary partner or spouse. This active "acting in" behavior is often going on at the same time the addict is acting out with herself or others.

An example of this sexual/intimacy anorexic behavior can be a woman who is avoiding or refusing to have sex with her husband, but is having an active masturbation life, affairs, or anonymous encounters. She is acting out her sexual addiction, but "acting in" her sexual/intimacy anorexia. Several female sex addicts will share their story of anorexia.

Intimacy Anorexia is what becomes of me once I am in a commit-
ted relationship. It's like I am unable to have intimacy and sex with
the same person. Intimacy and sex with the same person feels like
incest to me. As a result, my pattern has been to act out in illicit
relationships. All my life, I have run from the men in my life who
have sincerely loved and adored me. I always thought that this
feeling of incest was because they were not sexually satisfying, or
that I just "fell out of love" with them. My husband and I have just
recently entered therapy together on this issue. This will be the
first time I am not running away from a man who loves me. --Tina

I would avoid any real intimacy with people. I was afraid of letting
people get to know me so I used sex to form a bond, but with no
real intimacy or closeness. This is how my sex addiction masked
my sexual anorexia. I went out with two types of men - men who
were intriguing in some way, and usually another sex addict. That
fed the thrill seeking of my sex addiction of men who were safe and
stable, but sexually unattractive to me. I would alternate between
the two, and at the same time alternate between sexual addiction
and sexual anorexia. Either I was getting high from the intrigue of
the sex addictive relationship, or I was withdrawing sexually from
the "safe" relationship. In either case I was withdrawn emotion-
ally. I believe my emotional anorexia is the crux of either addic-
tion. I was not aware of this pattern until now. --Constance

I am not aware that I have ever had intimacy with a signifi-
cant other which would enable me to later pull away from him.
In most cases, I allowed boyfriends in my life because I was
lonely. But I don't recall caring for any of them on a deeper lev-
el, with the exception of my former fiancee. He seemed to care
for me a great deal. Perhaps my indifference towards him was
a form of anorexia. I think I have probably become unable to
bond with a man. I am not sure if that is because of the addic-
tion and the behavior or if that is the reason for the addiction.
--Abby

Anorexia for me is a three-part disease -- emotional, social, and sexual. I have been an emotional and social anorexic all my life. I have been constantly fearful of people and social situations. Emotionally withdrawn I used drugs and alcohol to numb myself to try to fit in. I acted out sexually (promiscuity) to get into one of the "safe" relationships where the sex addiction (acting out) yielded, and my sexual anorexia became operative.

In looking back I married into this relationship in hopes of controlling my sex addiction. All this did was turn the sex addiction inward and became sexual anorexic. I felt just as insane, if not more than when I was going insane, until I was directed (by my therapist) to read some books on sex and love addiction. I started going to SLAA and heard other peoples' stories. I had felt alone, ashamed, and horrified at times at the thoughts I would have. I felt guilty for not loving my husband sexually.

I left my husband knowing our relationship was dishonest. Since then I have stayed out of any kind of relationship for almost a year. I am now able to see more clearly my addictive behaviors. I know getting into a relationship to try to control an addiction, or to try to get over another relationship doesn't work. Today I am working on developing more intimate (without sex), honest relationship -- letting others get to know me and getting to know them with no strings attached. Also I am trying to acknowledge and express my feelings to others to help work through the emotional anorexia -- the crux of the problem for me. Having a higher power helps to give me the strength and courage I need to deal with these problems. My greatest supporter of my growing in a positive direction, becoming whole and happy, is my Higher Power. --Constance

Intimacy anorexia has only occurred for me when I got too emotionally/intimately close to another. The majority of my relationships have been lacking in the intimacy area (I tend to attract those type) — but I do know that when I did get close (felt dangerously close), I shut down completely sexually. I would still go through the motions, though. --Kittie

My counselor now tells me that I'm anorexic. I have been reading up on the matter. I find that I do fall into the characteristics of a sexual anorexic. This is difficult for me because I can't seem to shake it. I have been in recovery for this problem for a year. I don't know why it is so difficult to get past, but I wouldn't wish this (among other things) on anyone. It isn't the worst thing to be in the world, but it is hard to get through. I feel lucky to be in a support group of other women to help me. I know that I have a lot of work, but I will beat this feeling. I really just feel like I have no feelings for my husband. I resent him trying to be loving. I blame everything on him or others. I have always tried to avoid being addicted to anything. I don't experiment with drugs, don't over-consume alcohol, avoid caffeine, avoid nicotine; you know, all the things that everyone else has a problem with, I avoid. --Julie

I still struggle here. It isn't that I don't love my husband, but I still have a hard time seeing what he wants as exciting. I also have spells where any sex at all brings back thoughts that I don't want.

When I first started getting hooked on the pornography, I had a ravenous sexual appetite with my husband. I don't know if the pornography was a result of the overactive sex drive, or if it kicked in because of the pornography. I just know that it coincided. After a while, my husband just didn't measure up to the fantasy guy I had on-line. I began to make excuses for sex and spent all my time on-line so that I was up longer than, or going to bed before, he got home so I wouldn't have to be bothered. I would fake being asleep when he tried to initiate when he got in late. There was always a way out. Eventually my stomach would turn at the thought of being with him because he was so boring. --Rhonda

I think that because my husband was anorexic to me, it caused me to take on his behavior. I, too, became the same way. I basically gave up on sex. --Susan

I cheated on him numerous times. I never wanted to have sex with him other than in the beginning of the relationship. I would make excuses so I would not have to have sex with him. --Gail

Single people can be anorexic as well, but it will usually show up in patterns of having no relationships for years at a time, or many short-term relationships that never seem to quite work out.

While looking at some of the characteristics of sexual anorexia described on the following pages, it may be helpful to review the criteria to determine if spouses or significant others may have this issue as well.

There are nine characteristics that pattern intimacy anorexic behavior. The following characteristics can be reflected upon to determine if intimacy anorexia may be an issue. If the following characteristics apply, we would encourage you to read or watch Intimacy Anorexia which is available in the back of this book (See Appendix).

Characteristic One

This characteristic would include behaviors of staying so busy that there is little time left for the husband or significant other. Keeping so busy with the children's lives, various social events, church volunteer programs, or favorite television shows or books, that real intimate time with the spouse or committed relationship is actively avoided. If a spouse asks the anorexic to go out together, the anorexic may insist on bringing a child, friend, or in-law along. The anorexic believes that vacations are for families only, and not just for couples. Being alone with enough time to become emotionally intimate is consistently avoided.

One point can be given for those who answer yes to the characteristics described above.

Characteristic Two

If issues come up in the relationship of the anorexic, the spouse/partner is blamed before the anorexic looks at herself. The female sex addict who is an anorexic has no problems of her own. She has a good reason for everything she does. Even her acting out, or withholding behavior, is his fault. The dynamic "If he would just..." is simple. The anorexic can rarely see her own weaknesses. Often she has to be pushed into a corner before she will even acknowledge a fact she already knows is true.

One point can be given for those who answer "yes" to the characteristics described above.

Characteristic Three

Limiting or withholding love from the spouse or partner, such as saying "I love you" is part of Characteristic Three behavior. This is a hard characteristic for an anorexic to be honest about, because of the attitude "Look at all I do for him...the cleaning, dishes, and the children..." Yes, but what has been done loving toward **him** that is for **his** personhood directly to make him feel really loved?

One point can be given for those who answer "yes" to the characteristics described above.

Characteristic Four

Limiting or withholding praise from your spouse or partner is a part of Characteristic Four behavior. Every person deserves praise on a regular basis.

One point can be given for those who answer "yes" to the characteristics described above.

Characteristic Five

Limiting or withholding sexual intimacy from a husband or partner is another characteristic of acting-in behavior. This characteristic can manifest in the obvious way such as not having much sex, or no sex at all, with the spouse or partner. This can also manifest in not being emotionally present during a sex act so that he doesn't want to be sexual in the future. He is made aware that sex with him was not necessarily desired. Sexual anorexia is about the withholding the heart from a spouse or partner, not just withholding sex.

One point can be given for those who answer "yes" to the characteristics described above.

Characteristic Six

Controlling husband or partner around money is an issue for the anorexic. The anorexic can spend whatever she wants, but he had better check in before spending anything. If he spends, he is shamed for his selfishness, thoughtlessness, or how she could have gotten a better deal.

One point can be given for those who answer "yes" to the characteristics described above.

Characteristic Seven

The anorexic is unable or unwilling to discuss feelings with her spouse or partner. This applies to many female sex addictswhether they are anorexic or not. Almost all addicts are emotionally underdeveloped. If the addict didn't know what she felt, she acted out and felt better. This hardly equips her for emotional expression skills, or the ability to share her real feelings toward her husband or partner.

One point can be given for those who answer "yes" to the characteristics described above.

Characteristic Eight

Have ongoing or ungrounded criticism toward a spouse or partner is Characteristic Eight behavior. Feelings are present that he can't do anything right, especially if it's not done her way. He may be criticized for who he is, not only for what he does or doesn't do. This criticism can be used to spoil any close moments that could be shared. This criticism can be especially present on vacations, or long drive times, to make sure that the relationship doesn't move toward the sharing of feelings. Being critical can also be used to put off sexual advances. If he is made to feel mad or hurt, the last thing he will want to do is have sex.

One point can be given for those who answer "yes" to the characteristics described above.

Characteristic Nine

Controlling by anger or silence, especially when he is getting too close is a part of Characteristic Nine. When dealing with an imperfection of hers, she keeps him walking on egg shells so he will pay for talking about something she doesn't. The other side of this control is silence. The anorexic just won't talk about "it" and literally won't speak to him, and at all costs, avoid "it". Either silence or anger can be used to control him.

One point can be given for those who answer "yes"to the characteristics described.

Add up all the points that apply. Some probably can't resist applying these questions to husbands or partners as well.

If scores amount to 5 points or more, criteria for intimacy anorexia has been met. If both spouses scored 5 or more, this would mean both will have to do some focused work on sexual anorexia in recovery.

If intimacy anorexia is an issue, it will be important to get these needs met in a committed relationship, as opposed to fantasy and/or sexual acting-out behaviors. This can keep the addict from a binge-and-purge approach to recovery which goes like this: I don't act out sexually with myself or others, I don't have sex with my husband or partner: I eventually act out with myself or others in my sex addiction. Intimacy anorexia is difficult to address. I have treated female and male sex addicts and anorexics that do get and stay better. Having both journeys of recovery to make means acquiring skills that can bring a lifetime of spiritual, emotional, and sexual intimacy. In recovery love can be given in ways never thought possible.

Secret Cyberspace

Yes, the Internet has improved our lives in so many ways and yet in so many ways it hasn't. You can forgo going to the mall and getting your clothes, accessories, perfume and even the car you want to drive all by sitting at the computer.

However, there is a gross dark side to the Internet. This dark side of sex chat rooms, pornography, web camming and many other creative websites to lure the unfortunate sex addict into the candy of her choice. She can see profiles, pictures and even watch her potential next hook up perform his or her thing on another.

The Internet has brought to sex addiction what the mall has brought to the shopaholic. You now have a plethora of ways to escape your life, your past and medicate in a fantasy world of images and real events that have never been available to sex addicts any time before you. In this second edition of *She Has a Secret* we did an additional survey based just on the Internet. The 12 women who answered the survey all scored high enough on the Sexual Addiction Screening Test to qualify them as sexual addicts. Also, each person was called to verify that it was a woman that answered this survey. Although the numbers are small, I think it will give us a glimpse into the secret cyberworld that you may have experienced.

All of the names have been changed during this chapter for these ladies to keep their anonymity. If you would like to answer this survey, just email my office at heart2heart@xc.org or future research. Let's give you some basic information on this group of ladies.

The average age of these ladies is 40. They have a recovery date from 0 days to seven years. All the women who answered this survey indicated that they were heterosexual. These ladies marital status is:

42%   Married 1 Time
17%   Married 2 Times
 8%   Married 3 Times
 8%   Married 5 Times
25%   Never Married

Below are some of their responses to the survey on their usage of the Internet. The survey also asked them about some of their perceived consequences for this behavior in their life. As we have throughout this book we will include their comments to some of the questions as well. I know that this can help you see that other women have felt and experienced some of the same things you have in your secret world.

Below you will see that like yourself, they have used the Internet in several different ways to act out their sexual addiction. So each behavior listed is how the whole group responded to each item.

67%   Pornography
67%   Chat
42%   Web Cam
42%   Anonymous Encounters

The ladies also listed their use of erotica stories as part of their Internet usage. They also included cybersex as an activity they participated in when utilizing the Internet for sexual acting out. We asked these ladies to communicate in their own words as to why they used the Internet for sexual purposes. I think you will find their answers very similar to your own rationalization.

I started using the Internet when I was married. It was easier to meet men without going to a bar, etc. I quickly became addicted, signing on whenever my husband was gone. I rationalized that it was safer because you could not get an STD or run into a dangerous man if acting out on the Internet. I progressed to setting up sexual encounters and meeting men for sex. --Beth

I used the Internet to meet men and talk to them, I never went to meet them in person, just talked with them. --Sue

Secrecy! I could do it in private and no one would know about it. There were more choices any time that I wanted to do it day or night. There are more FREE choices so that people in my life didn't notice the expense. --Lisa

It was anonymous and I felt like I could explore and be whatever I wanted to be. I felt like I wasn't hurting anyone. It was a release and I found it soothing. Other times, I felt excited and secretive. I also used it to masturbate to. --Fran

It was an extension of my fantasy that there was someone better than my husband. I didn't know the person on the other side, so if I wanted to have someone who was caring, objectification I was feeling from my husband, someone who would rescue me from the objectification I was feeling from my husband, someone who turned out to be a sex addict. The Internet was somewhat like a "gateway" drug, that seemed harmless, could be justified, however, eased me into more risky behaviors that needed to continue in order for the fantasy to continue. --Vanessa

I could be whoever I wanted to be. I did not think I would have the courage to approach guys in person the way I did online. My shyness could disappear online. --Cheri

It was an easy access escape from my spouse who had stopped sleeping with me due to other problems in my marriage. It started out just looking at photos, then chats, then meeting with strangers. --Margaret

I can be anybody I want to be and live out any fantasy I desire. It's relatively safe...no one knows who I am or where I live and chances of being caught are slim. --Bobi

My husband used to travel and was active in his sex addiction (both porn and escorts) I know about the porn but not the other women. I believe I started using the Internet to medicate when we started to become disconnected. I told myself I wanted to meet someone new and start over, but I kept meeting addicts. I too have an addictive personality. --Taylor

Then we asked these women with a secret if they have had negative effects in their life due to using the Internet for sexual purposes. It's probably no surprise to you that 83% report having negative effects in their life due to this behavior. As we have throughout this book, we asked the ladies to give us examples of these negative effects they have experienced in their own life.

Because of someone I met on the Internet I divorced my husband and quit an online Masters program so I could spend more time on the Internet. --Beth

It made me feel cheap and dirty. I wanted to end my life several times but never could do it, for the fact I have 4 children. --Sue

Pop-ups; became a computer addict from it; it kept me behind closed doors and away from my family, which led to my divorce and the breaking up of my family in 2004...fortunately, i/we sought help and we are all back together going strong; and the worst of all...the pop-ups and "saved searches" were on my computer which my husband and daughter used and I got them addicted to pronography...secretly --Lisa

I went through a separation with my husband. I became suicidal and as very self-hating. I engaged in dangerous activities after meeting people online. I totally lost my sense of self. I compartmentalized so much that after awhile I couldn't keep up with my lies and "double" lives that I led. I told a lot of lies. I was extremely distant from my husband and family. I lived just to be on the computer. I gave up goals. I failed college classes as I was working at my masters at the time. I called off work just so I could be on the computer or out meeting people from the computer, or because I stayed up too late on the computer. --Fran

I feel like time was stolen from my work and my family, and that once the Internet was shut off I had to face the reality I was in, which was yet another abusive relationship, only this time I was married to the abuser. --Vanessa

Felt empty inside. --Anna

I lose track of time and end up being late for things like work. --Cheri

I wasted a lot of time and once I started using it to meet men I put myself at risk by going to their apartments and having unprotected sex. I didn't go to bars so the Internet was my one method of hookup. It was degrading and dangerous. --Margaret

The most negative effect is getting emotionally involved in the relationships that affect my work and family life. Not to mention the guilt and lack of peace that seems to keep me in an emotional turmoil. --Bobi

Loss of time with my children when they were younger. Loss of sleep. Stress. Loss of self esteem. --Taylor

After these conversations with these participants we ventured into surveying pornography. I know we talked a little about this earlier, but this is specifically addressing pornography on the Internet. Interestingly only 18% of our participants actually purchased pornography on the Internet.

We then asked if their appetite for pornography increased. Fifty-eight percent said that yes, their appetite for pornography has increased. Then we asked if the type of pornography has changed since they started on the Internet. Here are their responses to this question.

58%   Yes
17%   No
25%   Did not apply

Several of the ladies wrote a comment about the types of pornography they watched. If you feel this might trigger you, you can pass by their comments.

I did watch real people with a web cam and watched women masturbate on an adult website. --Beth

Going to different websites looking at pictures, printing pornographic stories in detail of how I wanted to be treated sexually and watching movies. --Sue

Originally stared with male sites, ultimately ended up on male/female hard core sites. --Lisa

Well, I don't look at pictures of porn so much, but I read porn. I started out interested in sex and then started investigating fetishes. --Fran

It started as just pictures that we received from a friend, then I would click on links. I would even go to the filter where emails were quarantined and click on the links. There was enough stimulation that I didn't need to purchase, but I wanted to. --Vanessa

Started with regular light things such as playboy then escalated all the way to looking for amateur bondage, aggressive sex, etc. --Cheri

Searching for the high

I started out just looking at men and got bored with normal stuff. I found assailants. It just kept getting worse. --Margaret

Only tried to meet men online. Wanted them to tell me I was attractive and my husband was crazy to cheat on me. --Taylor

Many female sex addicts start at an entry point on the Internet and progress to real people. So we asked these women to estimate how many people they had actually acted out with physically. Seventy-two percent of these women stated being sexual with someone via the Internet. Here are their responses to the number of people they believe they were actually sexual with, now remember most of these women are married already.

18%	0
9%	0-5
18%	5-10
37%	10-20
9%	20-30
9%	Over 50

We asked how they located those with whom they acted out with sexually. Here are some of their comments.

I first went to chat rooms with romance, or love titles. That progressed to chat rooms with sex titles. Later I used adult websites. --Beth

I used MySpace to find people in our area, however I never met any of them in person. --Sue

I chatted with them online and then met them in real life. --Fran

Actually started in an online poker site. We would chat at the tables, and it would lead to IMing. It would start casual conversations that would touch on inappropriate conversations to having "cybersex." There were almost quasi-relationships formed, as people would pair up with different poker partners.--Vanessa

Usually going into chat rooms or logging on to specific websites for sex. --Cheri

I never had to look. I kept ICQ on and I always had some guy request a chat which always led to sexual activity through chatting and sometimes an actual meeting. I was always amazed at how someone would be nearby even though I never even put my city down. --Margaret

I started playing multilayer games on the Internet not realizing you could actually talk to the people you played with. It's only through these games that I've met people. --Bobi

Through AOL messaging. Looking at their profiles. Started talking and being friends. They usually initiated it becoming sexual chat. Sometimes I feel like I let it become sexual to obtain "love" and affection. I've read since then that women do that. I wasn't looking for sex but didn't mind it either. --Taylor

There is with any addiction a cycle you go through to act out. Using the Internet in your sexual addiction would be no different. Your own cycle may be somewhat unique to you but I think you will identify with some of the cycles these ladies have experienced.

I would feel lonely and that I was ready to meet another man so I would search the Internet for a man then I would meet with him and have sex, even if I didn't want to after meeting them. I usually had a high for a while which later became fear, guilt and shame. --Beth

I felt wanted then I would get happy then excited, afterward I felt cheap. --Sue

the high

narcissistic *Like I was getting away with something then I would feel a rush then a disconnect to what I was doing completely with no regard to personal safety, emotional safety or anyone else at all afterward I felt ashamed and closed up my emotions from my husband even more. --Lisa*

I felt edgy and then I would act out on the Internet. Afterward I felt release. --Fran

I felt aroused then I would talk dirty then fantasize. Afterward I felt pursued. --Vanessa

I felt lonely then I would read erotic fiction then masturbate. Afterward I felt empty inside and even more lonely than before. --Anna

I felt depressed then I would go online then chat with guys afterward I felt guilty. --Olivia

I felt bad then good then bad, afterwards I felt sad. --Charlotte

I felt bored and lonely, very much alone. Then I would look for someone to chat with and end up somewhere sexual with it to make me feel more empowered and desired. Afterwards I felt like crap because typically those men were married and had just cheated on their wives with me. --Cheri

I felt alone then I would start searching for photos and stories. I would masturbate with or without chatting with someone else. Afterward I felt more alone then before. --Margaret

I felt very lonely or upset by something then I would get on the computer to see if anyone I knew was online and if not I would go look for someone. Afterwards I might feel okay for a short while but always ended up feeling like I don't know who I am, guilty, lost and still lonely. --Bobi

I felt lonely then I would look for new people to meet or contact ones I was already chatting with. Then I'd feel better when I heard what I wanted or miserable when I didn't or just exhausted from being up till 2-3 a.m. It was difficult to get up in the morning to get the children ready for school. It was crazy! --Taylor

the lie the tempo high

Often the addiction will lure you in with the excitement, risk, feeling powerful, beautiful, desirable like any addiction through there is the hangover or emptiness that goes with acting out. We specifically asked these sex addicted women to describe how they felt after they acted out.

There was an initial thrill from the accomplishment, a high. I felt as if I had accomplished a great feat. I was a woman!! This turned into shame and guilt, fear about contracting an STD. --Beth

It made me feel like someone that I did not deserve to be around, I would lie to my husband and my children daily. --Sue

A mixture of things...Ashamed, unfulfilled, wanting more, determined to stop. --Lisa

I felt different things. Sometimes I felt excited and couldn't wait for more. Other times I felt guilty and ashamed. --Fran

Lonely and empty. --Anna

Guilty, more depressed then before. Stuck in this addiction cycle. --Olivia

Usually very disappointed with myself. --Cheri

Disgusted and depraved. --Margaret

When I first began acting out, I felt high, excited but over time I just felt dirty, stupid and tormented by guilt, and very confused about my behavior. --Bobi

Sometimes better. Sometimes guilty. Sometimes used.Sometimes like a failure and disappointment to God. --Taylor

So how do these women protect themselves from the Internet now that they have started recovery? Here are some of their thoughts and afterward I will give you a couple of my own thoughts as well.

Probably not as much as I should, I just don't go to any of those sites. --Beth

I have deleted my MySpace account, all my past contacts from my email address book and replaced the sexual searching online with positive things like my homework, reading from the crime library, and such. I do whatever it takes to stay away from sexual behavior online. --Sue

I have set into place accountability partners who frankly have failed me... they get nervous and don't know how to deal with my calls because they can't relate with it as a result, they have pulled away as accountability partners. The only groups are men's groups in the area and I won't be in a room of men only talking about sex, it's not healthy for me! --Lisa

Nothing. --Fran

I removed the programs from my computer. --Vanessa

Stopped reading the erotic fiction. --Anna

Try not to go online after 10 p.m. Cancelled my accounts at online chat rooms. --Olivia

Kept myself accountable to others with my computer use. Stay away from my computer when I am alone. Pray, pray, pray. --Cheri

I've used accountability. I still have to use the Internet on a daily basis. I mainly stay off late in the evening or if I'm angry and I removed ICQ. --Margaret

Nothing really. I know I should, but I can't bring myself to do anything about it. --Bobi

Family filter. --Taylor

The Internet is a very dangerous place. I would highly recommend software that not only blocks porn, but has accountability software connected to it as well. This software emails those who are walking through this with you the exact pages you do visit. You can go to our website www.drdougweiss.com to try it.

If you are not in a group you might think about a telephone group by calling our office at 719-278-3708. You definitely will have a more successful recovery if you are in a group, especially if they are working through the *Secret Solutions* workbook together. If your addiction is involving sex with others, your self abandonment is significant enough to seek professional help.

Lastly, I asked the ladies what they would like to share with you from their experience of you are still using the Internet for your sexual addiction. Here is what they would like to say to you:

It scares me now to think of the danger I put myself in. That there is freedom out of the bondage of Internet addiction. --Beth

How unhealthy it really is, the chance of losing your family is not worth it. The risk that you take every time to go to meet someone. How to get your life back in control and not let the monster inside come back out to hurt you.--Vanessa

It's so easy to get sucked in. Using the Internet makes finding willing partners so easy. There were days that I didn't even leave the house, I just sat at the computer all day. It's not healthy and it's not going to help to break the addiction cycle. --Olivia

It is not good and you get hooked on it. It is hard to stop because you might seek this out instead of a relationship. --Charlotte

It is a hole that has no end to it. You will continue to go down further and further. When you do decide you want to be in a relationship it's hard because you have no trust. You cannot even trust yourself so how can you trust in a relationship? It just leads to an empty life where you have to fill your sexual addiction with another one in order to cope with what you are doing online (such as drinking). --Cheri

Reach out. You are not alone. I felt like I was the only woman who would look at such stuff. I'm not. --Margaret

Even though I still struggle, I've come to realize that it's all a fantasy that it's designed to entrap and keep you addicted. It makes real relationships pale in comparison and much more difficult. One time I heard that Satan offers us illegitimate ways to meet legitimate needs. I know that our needs are real and all part of being human. But I also found in my attempt to meet my needs through this behavior doesn't just affect me. I know many of the men I met just want the sexual encounter but I've met others who are just as lonely and in pain as I am. So now I am a user and abuser too. I have to realize that I'm playing games with real people's lives and I have no right to do that. --Bobi

To stop and look within to see what hope they are trying to fill. To pray for help. To be aware that language is very powerful and women are susceptible to that (i.e. romance novels). Listen to what we tell our children-that we can't REALLY know someone online. That we are trying to replace intimacy with intensity --Taylor

Ending the Secret

Five Principles for Recovery

I formulated The Five Principles for early recovery to be helpful for both female and male sex addicts. Recovery is similar to the healing of a broken bone. The bone needs the support of a structure to mend over time. The woman addicted to sex is in need of a structured recovery plan. If you can apply these principles of early recovery, it can make your journey through recovery much smoother. It is in my experience that those who use these 5 behavioral principles early on in recovery will tend to make the choice of ending this secret much simpler.

The most helpful thing I have done to help myself with this addiction includes reading books on the subject and attending on-line meetings on the internet. --Abby

An Early Plan For Recovery

There are some basic principles that can help sustain your successful recovery from sexual addiction. Early recovery is not simply understanding the facts, nor is it simply talking about sexual addiction. Recovery goes much deeper than talking about what was done in the past. The five principles are relatively simple to implement into your day-to-day activities. They can be used much like a checklist that you can put on a wall or mirror at home, where you can see it all the time. You may want to write the principles down and check them off as you complete them on a daily basis. This is an ideal behavioral checklist for the recovering sexual addict. It assures her that she is putting behavior toward recovery, rather than just coming to an understanding about sexual addiction.

Coming to an understanding is not the only answer for sex addicts. She may have been in pain for years and possibly repeated some addictive sexual behaviors hundreds of times. It is for this reason that the Five Principles, when put in place, give her an action plan, so she can begin to arrest the addiction she has been struggling with for so long.

Principle #1 - Morning Prayer

I have begun to be in conscious contact with my Higher Power. I feel a new freedom, sense of self and self respect. --Debra

Prayer is something that many sexual addicts find hard to do, especially if they have been avoiding God because of the shame and guilt of their behavior, or possibly because of what was done to them in the past. Prayer is simply a behavior that, when put in place, can change one's disposition.

We know from all of the other addictions studied, that an addiction is basically self will run riot. This expression of addiction simply means "doing your own thing." So the first thing in the morning, set aside time to pray. Don't do your own thing. Do Principle #1 instead.

Prayer, at this point, does not mean that you have to believe in God. It simply means to pray, and praying is talking. When the old timers in Alcoholics Anonymous went to their meetings, they didn't say, "Well if you believe in God, pray." They said, "Get on your knees and pray." Of course the knee thing is totally optional.

If you don't believe in God, talk to Him about it. You don't have to pray long. You can say, "God, I don't believe in You, but I'm supposed to pray. I want to recover. Would you help me stay sober today?" From that point on, you can also discuss any other issues that you want to talk to Him about. He is able to handle hurt, anger, fear, anxiety, or any other feelings or thoughts that you have kept from Him. Prayer is a way for you to behaviorally change yourself. See it as a positive step in your recovery.

Sexual addiction for many women addicted to sex starts early in the day -- not necessarily the first thing in the morning, but perhaps during the drive to work or dropping off the kids at school, etc. Prayer is preventative. It is a way of acknowledging that you are a sexual addict and are in desperate need of sobriety. Without sobriety, you are on a path of self destruction and you'll probably shatter other lives as well. More than likely, those around you have been devastated, either through your anger, depression, or acting-out behavior. As an addict, you are in a fight every day, especially the first 30 to 90 days of recovery. Remember, the first 30 to 90 days is one of the toughest periods of recovery for the sexual addict. Make sure you connect with God.

Prayer may or may not make you feel better instantly, but if you begin to apply it to your life, you will begin to reap the benefits. Prayer is one of the many new tools that you will have as a recovering person.

Principle #2 - Reading

Reading recovery material that is specifically related to sexual addiction is important. There are many books on the market you can read. It is very important to read some material every day. It is most beneficial to read in the morning. Addicts need to be reminded of what may be in store for them that day. Sometimes what you have read will come to mind in a difficult time. Those recovery thoughts can be the very tool to get you out of that tough situation, by giving you the strength to fight it. It is important to involve your mind in your recovery. Your mind alone will not save you, but it may help you so that you can maintain your abstinent behavior and not cross the bottom line you have drawn. A list of optional reading materials can be found in the Appendix of this book.

By now you probably have a feeling that your morning routine is going to change. These principles take five to fifteen minutes. They can make a dramatic change in your day. Remember, no matter what you've believed in the past, you are worth getting the recovery you need, so that you can restore yourself, your family, and your friends. You are going to learn a lot, not only about yourself, but about recovery in general. By doing so, you can successfully integrate into a life-style of hope.

Principle #3 - Go To Meetings

It has been good going to meetings because you know you are not alone. --Ivette

In Alcoholics Anonymous there is an old expression that many addicts apply to their recovery that says, "There are three times when you should go to a meeting: when you don't feel like going to a meeting, when you do feel like going to a meeting, and at 8 o'clock." It is not a matter of how you feel about it. It is how you behave about it.

In Twelve Step Meetings there is a "ninety meetings in ninety days" rule. This rule is ideal. I work with addicts all over the country through telephone counseling and I know that in most major metropolitan areas, there are meetings every day of the week.

Meetings are basically to support you, and at the same time give to others what you have learned through your own personal journey of recovery. Being around other recovering sexual addicts is going to encourage you. First, it is going to give you increased hope as you see other sex addicts have more sobriety. Secondly, you may believe that if they can do it, you can too. You can learn many things from others in recovery that they have learned through their own negative or positive experiences. I want to encourage you to go to as many meetings as possible.

Principle #4 - Phone Calls

Making a phone call can be the very thing that saves you from an acting-out experience today. The first step of the Twelve-Steps talks about the word "we." "We" means that you need someone else in your program to help you. In the past, "I" has been the biggest focus in your world. Before recovery you were powerless. In being powerless, you couldn't fight sexual addiction alone. You needed to involve others in the fight for sobriety. Having someone else involved dissipates the energy that comes against you. Sexual addiction can not be dealt with alone. I have not experienced, nor have I met anyone who has experienced, sexual addiction recovery alone and maintained not only abstinence, but a life-style of sobriety.

When you are not alone, then you are accountable. A life-style of sobriety is a much greater goal than just being abstinent.

There are several ways to address this principle of making phone calls. One way is to wait until you get into crisis and then call someone to help you. This method does not work, because if you don't have a relationship already established with anyone, you essentially have set up a barrier that isolates you from those that could possibly help you. To make a phone call and say that you are a sex addict is a big enough task to accomplish -- let alone calling someone you haven't established a relationship with and telling them of your plight. It's likely you won't make the call at all without a relationship already established.

The best way to utilize Principle #4 is to make one phone call in the morning to another recovering female sex addict, if you know one. If you don't know another recovering female sex addict, get the support of a strong spiritual person or a good friend (female) you can trust with your secret. Tell her that you are a recovering sexual addict, and you are not in trouble now, but if you get in trouble during the day, you are going to use the phone and call her back. By doing this you are checking in with someone. Eventually the phone calls will turn into conversations that develop into healthy recovery relationships. We all need relationships, and part of our resocialization is making phone calls, feeling connected, and getting acceptance right at the beginning of the day. If you can make a phone call early in the morning to someone else in the program, you will most likely find the strength you need to succeed in your recovery throughout your day.

Like prayer, reading, and meetings, the phone is a tool you can use to help yourself grow stronger, especially within the first 30-90 days when your need for other people to help is the greatest. The people you call will benefit just as much, if not more, when you call them. Make a phone call to someone else in recovery every day. Again, this principle, as well as the other principles we have already discussed, is very helpful when added to your checklist each day. You don't need to philosophically agree with this concept, or have a good feeling about it, to decide if you are going to do it. This behavior is designed to help you get sober today.

If you don't live in a metropolitan area, and can't get to meetings, it can be more difficult for you when you're in a tough situation. An alternative could be getting together frequently with someone you've met at a meeting. This will give you support and a relationship with someone who can help you. The bottom line is, however, you need to be in as many meetings as possible.

At this point, I would like to take a moment to explain why I emphasize attending meetings so much. I believe in <u>maximum</u> thinking. This is when you ask yourself, "How much can I do? What can I clear out of my schedule, especially for the first quarter of my recovery?" <u>Minimum</u> thinking is, "How little can I do? Can I possibly go to one meeting a week and be able to satisfy my husband or my own conscience?" Minimum thinking will really hurt you in the long run. If you decide you want to recover, you will need to hit it hard at the beginning. This is the best way to do it. Take an honest look at your schedule and remove those things that would interfere with attending meetings. Three months is a very short period of time to go every night that you can. If you need a listing of the meetings, the national numbers are in the appendix of this book. It is important to meet frequently with other female addicts if you can. There are also on-line recovery meetings, if you don't have any in your local area.

This principle of attending meetings was established with Dr. Bob and Bill W. in the founding of Alcoholics Anonymous. For information on the development of support groups you can get the video called *My Name is Bill W.* starring James Garner. You will be encouraged by how these principles have worked for more than 70 years with addicted people worldwide. We can help one another if we can get together. If you isolate yourself, you can't be helped, nor can you help others. Some days you will be the one needing the help, and on other days you'll be helping other sex addicts, which is a great feeling. That is sobriety. When you give that gift away, it reinforces your own recovery. Now I know many of these meetings are attended by men. You will probably be able to get the phone numbers of some women who are in recovery. Call our office for telephone groups.

Principle #5 - Pray Again

This may sound like it will take a lot of effort and it will. You can read Principle #1 again to be reminded that this is not something you have to like or agree with. It is something you just have to behaviorally do. At the end of the day, if you are sober, thank God for keeping you sober that day. Sobriety isn't something you do by yourself, it is something you do with the help of God and others. If there are any other issues from the day that you want to talk to God about, you can bring them up at this time. If you don't have a relationship with God, ask Him to deepen your relationship with Him, and to send people to you to bring this relationship about. It is important to end your day in a spiritual place in addition to starting the day this way.

The recovery program that is going to work is spiritual in nature. So, it is important to reestablish your own spirituality since you were born a spirit, with a soul, living in a body. While most addicts give attention to their souls (their mind, will, and emotions) and their bodies, they usually don't nurture their spiritual component. Make this a time of being thankful that you had a day of sobriety today. Even the worst day in sobriety is something to be thankful for, because even on the best day without recovery, you were covered with shame, guilt, and fear.

So, if you have any relief from those feelings, I believe it is appropriate to thank God in prayer.

Tips For Finding a Twelve Step Group

Unlike other addiction support groups such as Alcoholics Anonymous and Narcotics Anonymous, Sex Addict's Twelve Step support groups vary. There are several groups to choose from, and all over the country they vary from region to region, and within regions as well.

The three major groups for sexual addicts are Sex Addicts Anonymous, Sexaholics Anonymous, and Sex and Love Addicts Anonymous. These three groups make up the majority of sexual addiction Twelve-Step groups. These three groups interface differently in different parts of the country.

Optional

In your search for a support group, you can try any of these three Twelve Step groups. A broad generalization is that Sexaholics Anonymous is generally known to be more like an Alcoholics Anonymous program in which a slip is a slip and is acknowledged as such. In Sex Addicts Anonymous there appears to be more tolerance of behaviors, generally speaking. Sex and Love Addicts Anonymous deals more with the love addiction component regarding chasing relationships and trying to be fixed by people in your life. This group, however usually has more women in it, and you may find that helpful for a sponsor and accountability. Because these groups vary, any one group may or may not deal with the sexual compulsive part of the addiction. This is an important distinction. If someone is mostly a sex addict, they need to be in a group that deals specifically with the compulsive behavior of sexually acting out.

My encouragement would be to find the Twelve Step groups in your area. Pick one that addresses sexual compulsive behavior.

If you are limited to only one group in your area, then you don't have much of an option. I still encourage you to attend.

You'll have to work around whatever it is that the particular group is lacking, but you will still benefit from everything else the group can offer. What you will need from the group as a recovering sex addict is a point of identification with others. Just knowing that others in the support group know what you're dealing with when you say, "You know what I mean?" makes all the difference. They know the pain, shame, guilt, and fears you have walked with, and can appreciate the courage it takes to be honest. There is a lot more shame and guilt included in this particular addiction compared with other addictions. Any group is going to be better than no group.

Sex addicts need a place to be honest. Honesty is going to be a new skill for those who have mastered being dishonest and have lived two different lives. In your support group, you can begin to practice sharing things that you have never shared before and get a positive response for being honest, especially from people who know what it is taking you to break through.

Encouragement is another thing needed from the group. Encouragement comes in various forms. It may come in the form of one person working their recovery successfully, and another person being able to say, "Wow, that's something I want to have." This type of encouragement happens frequently in Twelve-Step support groups.

It is encouraging when you work on your recovery to the point where it inspires others. There is a lot of work that is to be done in the Twelve Step groups. When one person does the work, it encourages others to work on their own recovery.

Feedback is crucial for the sexual addict. When you are in denial, you are unable to feel and connect with the pain you may have caused others, or even caused to yourself. Sometimes getting feedback from others can help you get in touch with some of the pain that you have been running from.

Feedback can also help some of the cognitive thinking or what they call in Alcoholics Anonymous "stinking thinking," and get you into sober thinking. It can also challenge some behaviors and establish boundaries. The feedback portion of the group will happen at what is called "check-in-time." After the meeting, the leader of the group may say "Does anyone want to check in?" This is when you will share where you really are in your recovery, get honest with two other people, and get feedback if you want it. Other people who have been where you are can help you get through and get what you want in your recovery. Feedback can help quite a bit.

When you attend a Twelve Step meeting, make sure you get a phone list from the group, if they have one, or approach a couple of people after the meeting and ask them for their phone numbers. Having phone numbers of other recovering sex addicts when you need them is crucial to your personal recovery. Practice making phone calls to other **female** members in the group on a daily basis. This is the safety net for your early recovery. Phone calls can ultimately save you from a future relapse.

Another benefit of your support group is spirituality. As you look at the Twelve Steps (We'll go over these in a later chapter.), you will notice that God is mentioned quite a bit. Some addicts may not have been able to connect with God, because of the guilt and shame of their own behavior. Some may have had a relationship with God but because of the addiction, they were living incongruent with their relationship to God and now feel distant. In a support group, you will see some people with the same faith, who begin to piece back their relationship with God, and begin to see a serenity in living congruently with what they know to be true.

You also will see those who listen to their intuition. When they know they are in danger, they won't act out. You will hear about some addicts praying and getting alleviated from a current situation that they needed help with, so that they could stay sober. Spirituality is more often caught than taught. As you go to Twelve Step meetings, you will begin to catch the flavor of spirituality and add it into your life in such a way that it makes sense. God makes sense when we see someone across the room getting help. We know then that He can probably help you, too. If God can provide the things necessary in the program, then you can probably expect to get some positive results. You will find that God isn't some mystical, far-away Being, but rather quite practical and relational. Through the group, you will receive something that you may not know that you need -- unconditional love.

Unconditional love is something we rarely get in our lives and when we do get it, it changes us. Unconditional love is often a part of Twelve Step groups. The other addicts in the group have been where you are, and they are loved by others that have been there. And now that you are there, you can receive the love that they have for you. They know that after you have done your first step, they will also know all of your secrets. As one old-timer said, "It sounds like you are one of us." The acceptance and unconditional love you will receive from this group is something you may not have known you needed. It will feel like a weight has been lifted off you when unconditional love comes your way. Many sex addicts have not been loved for who they really are. The group is a place where you can be unconditionally loved because they know you and accept you, just like you are.

Boundaries in support groups are very important. Some women without good boundaries will be susceptible to acting out with men in the group. If this does happen, be honest with the group. If this happens more than once you may need to attend a support group like CODA (Codependency Anonymous) and do your recovery work with women in that group if you cannot keep your sobriety in a mixed-sex recovery group.

Practicing these Five Principles and attending group meetings can allow you to see others who are achieving healing from their secret. My hope is that you can give this to yourself and inspire the others who are on their way to ending their own secret.

Body Healing

Body healing is a very import aspect for most women addicted to sex. Sex addicts have had biological and neurological training, and conditioning that went on within their body as well as their brain during their addiction. In this chapter when I discuss the brain, I am not talking about the thought life of the woman who is a sex addict, but the gray matter that is between our ears, the actual organ that has its own biological needs, development, and conditioning.

Similar to other muscles in your body that can be conditioned, you can condition your brain. We discussed how the brain of a sex addict actually evolves through releasing sexually in an altered-state experience. This can become the primary way in which the brain gets its chemical needs met. Therefore it is important to look at the healing of this facet of sexual addiction.

This is often an overlooked aspect of healing and it is for this reason we placed it first in this section. I firmly believe that the body is an integral part of the recovery process. I have witnessed too many women addicted to sex who did not take their body seriously, and relapsed because of their lack of respect for what had been going on within their body and brain for many years before they started recovery. It is for this reason we are going to look at this from what may seem like a detached perspective. We need to look at what happened to the brain while in the midst of an addiction.

In your addiction, you may have conditioned your body and sexuality to certain stimuli such as pornography or fantasy and released sexually while in that state. Let's look at the conditioning process. You go into a fantasy and start "cooking" it. This is the cue from a conditioning process that we will label "A."

"A" will lead you to the addiction cycle and you will pursue the behavior. The behaviors we'll call "B" will send "C" (the endorphin and enkephalin chemicals) to your brain. In your brain there is very little distinction between "A" and "C". The brain, as an organ, notes that you are starting to cook something and knows what behaviors are going to follow, and that "C" is going to happen next. This is the simple process in which you may have conditioned yourself many times.

You may be unaware of this conditioning, and that it feeds off itself and becomes stronger and stronger with repetition. It is important to look at this conditioning since it is so powerful. Anyone who is married knows that conditioning is powerful. If every time that you washed dishes you got a reward, you would never have to be asked to do them. It would be a conditioned response. We are creatures of conditioning and this can be worked to our advantage or disadvantage. In addiction, it works towards our detriment. In recovery, we can turn it around to also work toward our benefit. How can you recondition yourself as it relates to your sex addiction? The reconditioning process will work similarly in the fashion of "A" to "B" to "C."

When you start having sexually inappropriate thoughts, and for newly recovering sex addicts this will be frequently, put a rubber band around your wrist. Every time you have an inappropriate thought, snap the rubber band on the inside of your wrist. When you snap the rubber band, "P" will happen, which stands for pain. It will take about 30 days for this process to take the reconditioning effect. Some say a positive thought, after snapping the rubber band. Neurologically, when you get an inappropriate thought, your body is going to start associating it with pain. Most clients report to me that within a month of this reconditioning behavior, 80 percent of their sexually inappropriate thought life disappears. At this point most are ecstatic!

This fantasy life has been a part-time job for most women addicted to sex. Now they have just increased their productivity at work or in their relationships to about 15-20 hours a week! It is enjoyable to have your thoughts more under control and not have your time taken away by your fantasies. Reconditioning is vital for healing the body.

Another aspect, from a biological perspective, is accountability. Being accountable with your time, thoughts, and sexual behaviors is crucial. Finding someone to be accountable to brings into play a very important behavioral conditioning process. The pain of telling someone that you acted out is far greater than the pleasure of acting out. For this purpose it is important not to have your spouse be the person you are accountable to. It is important to be accountable to someone of the same sex. Accountability prepares a reconditioning experience. It is not an experience you want to repeat again and again. Eventually this accountability will set up a reconditioning process for your sex addiction recovery.

Many times sex addicts have rationalizations for their sexual behavior. For example, "My life is a mess, I deserve it," or "I'm so stressed out." These rationalizations can lead her back into her behavior creating more secrets and pain.

To recondition this behavior you can write a therapeutic letter about how you feel after you act out. Include in your letter the feelings of guilt, loneliness, despair, or hopelessness and the pain that you feel. Pick the worst situation that you can imagine in your sex addiction and include it in this letter. Now say aloud one of the thoughts that pulls you into your acting-out behavior. For example: "Just one more time, then I'll stop." After you say this, read the letter. Repeat this two times, twice a day for about a week. This will do the exact opposite of what your addiction has done. In your addiction you have conditioned your thought "Just one more time" to equal acting out (brain cookies). This was conditioned. Now after this exercise you have taken the same process and used it for your benefit. You begin to connect those words to pain. You will begin to associate this thought process with discomfort instead of a reward. Being the creatures that we are, we try to avoid pain, therefore, this will work for your benefit.

As we discussed in the chapter on biological aspects of sex addiction, some people may be depressed. Their brain, for whatever reason, does not produce enough endorphins or enkephalins to make them feel normal. The addict therefore has learned to modify her neurological balance through the burst of endorphins and enkephalins when she acts out, which make her feel normal. This may be the only time she feels this way. Once the person who is biologically depressed gets into recovery, she may move into a deep depression, characterized by not sleeping, sleeping all the time, not eating, eating constantly, energy loss, feeling worthlessness or hopeless, or she may be even having suicidal thoughts.

This is not the norm, but it does happen to some sex addicts beginning in recovery. This tells me that there is a biological depression that preceded the addiction and has been one of the major agents why the sex addict is in her addiction. Unfortunately, because of the solution that she chose to fix her brain's chemical imbalance, she needs now to recover just the same as any other sex addict. She still needs to work The Five Principles and to be accountable. Taking medicine will not cure the defects in the developmental dwarfing because of the addiction.

A biological depression is going to need a biological solution. The biological solutions available today far exceed anything we have known so far in the history of medicine. There are many antidepressants that psychiatrists recommend. The biological depression will not get better with spiritual or psychological application. If you had a bullet wound, you would need a doctor to take care of it. The woman addicted to sex who is biologically depressed needs not only the recovery steps we've discussed thus far, but also a biological solution, such as antidepressants and the care of a physician.

Soul Healing

There are several objectives to follow to heal the soul (mind, will, and emotions) of a female sex addict. In this chapter, we will discuss the process for healing the soul. The first process deals with the psychological dependency in sex addiction. The sex addict often becomes psychologically dependent on her addiction. This is generally the first place she discovered she could have her needs met in her sex addiction.

Psychological Dependency

A helpful tool to curtail psychological dependency is to write a thank you letter and a good-bye letter to your sex addiction. You will need to look at what your addiction has done for you. It has often kept you from being responsible or intimate in relationships, justified you leaving relationships, kept you feeling powerful, loving, always in control, and successful in your addiction.

In your thank-you letter, also thank your sexual addiction for what it has done for you from your adolescence, early adulthood, all the way through to the present. This will give you a good understanding of the psychological dependence you have had on your addiction in the past.

The next step is to write a good-bye letter. This will give you a point and time of when you confront the psychological dependence. This has actually been a relationship that you have had. It has been a real person that you have clung to in your fantasy world. Some have even crystallized this person. It is now important to face the psychological dependence of your sex addiction so that you can also confront the issues. From this letter you may be able to deduce some of the other issues that you will need to deal with.

If the dependence was for escape or entertainment, you are going to need to look at those issues and make a plan for legitimately meeting those needs in an appropriate manner. We do need to have fun, entertainment, and be loved in a healthy way. Your sex addiction was there often times to compensate for those needs not being met. In recovery, it will be your responsibility to identify these needs and find a healthy process of meeting them. The first aspect for healing the soul is to deal with the psychological dependency. This letter will be a beginning for this.

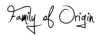 Family of Origin

For many addicts, their family of origin is a complicated issue. A majority of the women addicted to sex grew up in homes that were very dysfunctional. They may have been dysfunctional in many different ways. The family could have been neglectful to where they weren't praised, celebrated, or invested in. Another way the family may have been dysfunctional is that there were other addictions in the family such as food, nicotine, work, or sex which would make the environment that they grew up in very distant and emotionally absent.

In our study we asked female sex addicts about how their family of origin handled sex.

In my family we talked about sex in a positive manner.

96%   No
4%   Yes

In my family of origin we did **not** talk about sex.

83%   Yes
17%   No

Children from this kind of environment grow up without skills to deal with life's stresses or issues in a healthy manner. The child is then left to decide which addiction they will choose to medicate the absence of those skills and/or the pain of the distance within the family.

Also, an angry or more volatile family system can produce an addictive person. Abandonments could be part of the family of origin which includes divorces, where one of the parents leave. The child is then more susceptible to psychological pain, which is one of the pain agents for an addiction.

As you look at your family of origin, you may find the actual causes for issues you are dealing with. How did your parents deal with anger? Did they show love? In this chapter we will just highlight some of the soul aspects that need to be addressed during treatment. Individual therapy may be needed while looking at these issues. If there is a lot of pent-up anger related to your family of origin, it will show up in either the form of depression or hostility toward mom or dad, and this should be addressed during your treatment. Anger is held within your body and keeps you in pain. From the soul aspect, to recover from sex addiction, you will have to heal your mind, will, and emotions that are hurting because of neglect, abuse, or dysfunctional behavior in your family of origin.

On the other hand, some sex addicts grew up in an ideal situation. They are biological sex addicts who don't have family-of-origin issues to deal with.

But they will still have other issues to work on that we will read about later.

Feelings

Feelings are a major part of sexual addiction recovery. During your development years, many did not learn to identify or communicate feelings, and yet feelings can be one of the most treacherous and dangerous areas of early recovery. Many women addicted to sex have at some point felt unloved, rejected, or unappreciated, which places them in a difficult situation if they don't know how to express their feelings. Many addicts end up medicating these unknown feelings in an unhealthy way such as with sexual activity. This is just a lack of a particular skill issue. It is not a matter of a level of intelligence.

In the midst of her addiction, when the female sex addict had a feeling, and didn't know what it was, when she acted out, it went away. It was a simple solution. But in her recovery, she doesn't have this solution any more for her lack of feelings, and is no longer able to medicate by acting out. Now she has the problem of having a feeling and not knowing what it is.

The following exercise can help facilitate this emotional development. It is called *The Feeling Exercise*.

1. I feel _____ (feeling) when _____.

2. I first remember feeling _____ (feeling) when _____.

This exercise is difficult at first. It's like learning a new computer program. Although it may be frustrating at first, eventually you will get familiar with it, and then wonder how you ever lived without it. First we identify the feeling. Without doing this part of the exercise, you can't do the second part, which is communicate. In the appendix, you will find a feelings list. Pick a feeling word from the list and fill in the blanks.

For example:

1. I feel calm when I go to the lake.

2. I first remember feeling calm when I was laying on the grass with my sister on a farm making shapes out of the clouds that were passing by.

In this example, I am giving a picture. These are to be very specific experiences. What we are doing is creating files. Our emotions as sex addicts are similar to a messy desk. We are taking the papers off the desk in this exercise and putting them in a filing system that goes a, b, c, d... In computer language, it's like having a data base without file names on the data base. If we look for a file, we can't find it. This makes the addict feel like she doesn't know what to do, think, or feel, and so she acts out. Being able to identify feelings is very important. Do this exercise daily for a couple of months (or more if you want), so that your emotional language increases. Write them down and you will be able to experience your feelings. After your first 30 days of abstinence, you are going to find yourself having more feelings. It is important to realize what you are feeling so that you don't relapse.

The second part of this feeling exercise is communication. You can do this exercise with a therapist or with someone in your recovery group. You will need to communicate the feeling sentences that you have completed. I encourage you not to do this over the phone. You may want to do this exercise with your partner or spouse. It is important if you do this with your partner or spouse, that you do NOT use your relationship in any way, shape, or form as examples.

An example of what <u>NOT</u> to do:

I feel <u>frustrated</u> when <u>you don't pick up your socks</u>.

You can feel frustrated when you drive down the highway, or when the dog sleeps in your favorite chair, but don't aim the feeling of frustration at your partner, and don't use the word "you" otherwise it will lead to another way to battle each other.

If this exercise is done correctly, it can provide a safe place for you to communicate your feelings. While one person is sharing their feelings, the other one can listen. The person listening shouldn't make comments on the feelings shared for 72 hours afterwards. This creates a security for both to know that they are safe to communicate their feelings. This exercise will accelerate moving you from feeling frozen to thawed. This exercise will be like sitting in the microwave emotionally. Without this exercise, I find the sex addict seems to have more relapses, and it also takes a lot longer period of time to develop intimacy; which we will discuss next.

Intimacy

In early recovery, you were probably unable to become intimate because your feelings were still frozen, and you didn't have the skills necessary to be intimate. Intimacy is the result of having feeling skills and emotions. Because you have been medicating your emotions for so long, they are underdeveloped. You are really unable to develop the kind of intimacy that a lot of people experience. If you are in recovery, intimacy is an obtainable goal for your future.

Intimacy is basically the ability to be able to share your heart, feelings, or the deeper part of yourself with another human being. You will sense feelings of acceptance and love mutually. It has sort of a spiritual aspect to it. You will feel connected, close, and warm. Sex addicts, in their development, have learned not to share with people because of a lie they believe: "If you knew me, you wouldn't love me." Consequently, many sex addicts have not experienced intimacy, and therefore, don't believe that it exists. They need to grow past this.

You can practice intimacy and get better at it. This takes months, but as you practice sharing and being honest, you will experience intimacy. You'll begin to add to your healthy experiences and the more experiences you have, the more you will believe and accept the existence of intimacy. This is an integral part of the healing process.

Trauma

Trauma is a familiar event for most sex addicts. It may have been emotional, spiritual, physical or sexual abuse, and/or neglect. Trauma comes in many shapes, sizes, and forms. It is a very important piece in your soul's recovery. In this book, we are unable to go into great detail about trauma, since it could be an entire book unto itself.

Victims of trauma, abandonment, and/or neglect have to work through trauma issues, but it is quite healing to do so. After about 45 days clean in recovery, I find my clients are ready to work on their trauma issues. You will need to have your feelings in place before you can deal with trauma.

There are helpful techniques you can practice to address trauma. First identify what your trauma was. As you go through your feelings, you may go through some recall of what has been traumatizing to you. If your feelings have been frozen, you may not realize what actually was trauma, but as you thaw out your feelings in your recovery, trauma may become more obvious to you. As you complete Steps Four and Five, more information will lead you to believe there has been trauma in your life.

When you identify the trauma, make a list of the incidents so that you know what you are going to be dealing with. You may need a competent professional to help you through your trauma issues. It may be helpful to read the section on how to find a therapist for this issue. There are cognitive exercises as well as writing exercises, to work through your trauma.

I believe if you deal with trauma early in your recovery, your recovery will be more successful. Trauma work is essential for successful sex addiction recovery. Without it, you keep your soul in pain. With that pain, you keep the drive to medicate within you. You are worth recovery, and having the best life possible. But you will need to open up the secrets you have kept inside. If you have secrets, it may be that they are trauma secrets. Secrets can keep you sick and in your addiction. If you are keeping a trauma secret, it is important that you become honest. Many female sex addicts have been sexually abused by older women or men, and don't identify it as sexual abuse. Clients in my practice who could not acknowledge it as abuse, have increased the possibility of relapses during their recovery considerably. Once you have identified these traumas, you will want to begin working on them.

Spiritual Healing

When I am acting out, or am in fantasies, I am not connected to my Higher Power. I was not able to live in reality. Reality is not so bad if I live in the moment where God is. Sex addiction was a major block between me and God. --Constance

I had made sex my God. I had no spiritual life. I was driven by the addiction. --Debra

In our study of female sex addicts, it was truly overwhelming how much sex addiction robbed them of their spiritual life. Ninety-two percent stated that their spirituality suffered greatly. Another 8% stated that their spirituality suffered moderately. That represents every woman in our study. No one stated that their spirituality did not suffer, or that this did not apply to her. Spirituality greatly suffers because of sexual addiction.

On the flip side of how greatly female sex addicts felt their spirituality suffered is also the fact of how much their spirituality increased during recovery. Fifty-four percent stated that their spirituality increased greatly during their recovery from sexual addiction. Thirty-three percent in our study reported that their spirituality had increased moderately. Again, no one stated that their spirituality decreased, although 13% did state that this no longer applies to them at this point and time in their recovery. It can then be concluded that recovery from sex addiction **will** improve the area of spirituality in your life.

This means a majority of female sex addicts prior to being in recovery felt spiritual distance, but as they moved along in their recovery they once again felt their spirituality begin to grow.

So, no matter what your present spiritual status is, it can return once again to what it was or even deeper. Results from our study of women who had a spiritual background while growing up reported that 60% were Protestant and 20% were Catholic.

Because of these results, I feel the need to address some spiritual issues. If you are practicing another faith you can still make similar applications. I simply cannot give every religious practice equal time in the interest of space. The Bible has many examples of female sexual addiction although I can't recall a sermon on it, or a book written about female sex addiction from a religious point of view. Did you know that one of Jesus' closest female friends was a female sex addict that was set free by Jesus? Did you know that this female sex addict was the first person Christ appeared to after His death in His resurrected state?

Yes, it is true Mary Magdalene was a prostitute driven insane by her sexual addiction. She participated in selling her sexuality for money. She had many, many lovers and participated in many sex acts. But Jesus not only delivered her (in her case it was a spiritual-based addiction - longing to fill the void of God with sex) but He also befriended her. This clearly is a true picture of how I believe God (whatever you're understanding is of Him) loves and befriends female sex addicts.

Remember that this God loves you even though you had an active, sexual fantasy life. I do believe that the story of Mary Magdalene also points to the importance of continuing to grow spiritually. Mary did not take her freedom from Jesus and walk away from Him, rather she stayed close to Him and became a regular, daily follower of Jesus.

She listened to Him teach; she saw the miracles. I am sure she helped out in His ministry in practical ways. She became a friend to the core group of Jesus' followers. I think this is a great picture of the importance of daily spiritual growth and of staying in the presence of spiritually like-minded people.

In our study, associating with other spiritual people was evident in female sex addicts by their attendance of religious and spiritual meetings. These women answered whether they attended religious or spiritual meetings **while in the midst of their addiction.**

24%   Attended weekly or more
12%   Attended monthly
 8%   Attended a few times a year
56%   Did not attend

Looking at the same group of female sex addicts who now have experienced some sexual recovery, the numbers change significantly. The following are the answers to the same question regarding attendance of religious or spiritual meetings during their recovery.

46%   Attend weekly or more
13%   Attend monthly
 8%   Attend a few times a year
25%   Did not attend
 8%   Does not apply

As you can see this same group of women who have obtained some sexual recovery change the numbers significantly. I think that similar to our Biblical example of Mary Magdalene, the results of our study show that being around spiritually-based people is good for recovery.

What role does church play in your recovery? The answer has two primary variables. The first variable is your personal religious and/or church experiences, and whether they were favorable or less than favorable. The church or religious group itself, that you may be looking at for support, is the second variable.

Some churches, regardless of their denominational affiliation, are dysfunctional. Some of the dysfunctional beliefs found in churches are:

• Nobody here has a sexual problem.
• We don't talk about sexual issues.
• It is just sin, so repent.
• Honesty and humanity are not acceptable.

Notice that I said some churches are this way. But there are other churches who believe:

• Church members can have sexual issues.
• We can talk and heal through these issues.
• Sexual behavior can be addictive.
• Honesty and humanity are acceptable and appreciate here.

Finding a healthy church or spiritual group can be very positive for your recovery. Our study showed that 42% of the female sex addicts believed that the church or religious group they attended had been instrumental in their recovery.

Some tips on how to find a church or spiritual group follow. This is a trial-and-error process since it may take time to find one that works for you. As they say in recovery, take what you can and leave the rest!

Hints to finding a healthy church:

• They have counselors on staff.
• They have support groups for addictions.
• They have 12 step-type approaches to recovery.

Support found in a church may be less structured than a specific support group for female sex addicts. The support may come through a spiritually mature woman who can provide support, accountability, and a genuine care for you.

If a church does have a Christ-based sex addict support group for men such as a Freedom Group, they will often be just for men. Some men are opposed to women in the group, and others just feel awkward about it. In an earlier research study I offered for pastors regarding sexual addiction, I found that 84% of the pastors would be open to have a Twelve Step type support group if a church member led the group. If your pastor will let you have a group for just women, whether it's a female Freedom Group, or some other cloaked title such as "For Woman Only" or "Sexual Healing Group", this would be ideal. You can call other pastors and therapists from other churches to let them know about your group. You can also list this in most calendars of events or support group listings in your local newspaper. Remember to have them call the church about the group first, before you give out the location.

Grieving

When I came face to face with what I struggled with, the first stage for me was actually "relief." I finally understood what was up with me. When I identified my abuse, I identified my addiction. I was in denial about both for a long time, then I had a lot of sadness and anger, mixed in with a huge amount of shame for a long, long time. After almost 6 years of consistently working on my stuff, I am finally to the stage of accepting and actually admitting to others that I really struggle with sexual addiction. --Margaret

Grief is natural. It is a God-given process which human beings work through to naturally move through pain. The pain of the death of a loved one is often overwhelming. The process of grief allows us to take the pain in increments or stages. We will cover the grief stages, but first we will discuss how sex addicts grieve. Sex addicts do go through the grieving process during their recovery.

As the woman addicted to sex recovers, she grieves over her sexual addiction. Sexual addiction is a multifaceted relationship. It is a psychological relationship. Often your sexual addiction has been there for many years. It has been there to run to and nurture you, and it has been your primary route to false intimacy. It often was the first sexual experience.

So sexual addiction is often a loss of a relationship that you can no longer have. Sometimes it is the loss of a best friend. Losing your best friend can be painful. In all honesty, all of your relationships before recovery are usually secondary relationships. Your secret life was primary. When you count up the hours, you will find that sex addiction has absorbed thousands of hours of time. To say good bye to a friend who has been there all this time is difficult. Non-addicts or co-addicts will not understand this relationship, just like others don't understand what it is like to lose a parent unless they have gone through it themselves.

While going through the grief of losing a primary relationship, you may not meet a lot of people who understand, unless they are people in your Twelve Step group who have also gone through the grief and loss of a significant relationship. Your new life-style without your addiction can be very scary. The grief stages are a way to help you experience the pain of your loss and move on a little at a time. By moving through it successfully, you can enjoy the rest of your life with your primary relationships, such as your husband and children.

The Loss of Your Image

Your image is what you presented to the world. For a sex addict that is about 90 percent of her life. The addict projects an image of sometimes being very competent, strong, intelligent, success-ful, and a great wife. Often there is over-compensation for being an addict. You may feel you have to be more than human, so you project this perfect image to your peers, co-workers, family, and friends. It is the way that many sex addicts use to cope and hide their sexual addiction. Losing an image that you have crafted and perfected is quite a large loss.

The loss of self can be felt just as much as the loss of your addiction. You will also feel the loss of who you were to the outside world, and redefine that loss through recovery.

The Loss of People

You may have related with other sexual partners outside of your primary relationship. The losses of some of those relationships can be very painful. Indeed, you have over idealized your sexual relationships, and in your early recovery, it is going to be very difficult to separate the fact that your relationship was based on sex. The loss of places that you may have gone to is also a part of the losses you will feel in recovery, since you may have received social reinforcement there in your previous acting out days.

These are losses you will incur early in your sexual addiction recovery because you have depended upon these structures in your addiction to survive. I use the term "survive" and not live, because a sexual addict has only just begun to live as she enters recovery. In a lot of ways she has only experienced a limited amount of what life has to offer her.

Grief Stages

The stages of grief have been outlined by Koogler Ross as she worked with those who were dying of cancer. These stages have been applied to many aspects of life such as losing loved ones due to death, divorce, or injury. Loss of a primary relationship, such as when a sex addict loses her addiction, is important to discuss so that you know what to expect in recovery.

Stage One - Shock

I was so shocked at how powerful this disease is, especially with the mental obsession. Even though I had quit, the mental obsession was still there going strong. --Constance

Shock is a feeling you experience when you are initially confronted with a painful reality, such as acknowledging you are a sex addict. The first time it was mentioned to you, for a moment you may have felt a realization of "What am I doing?" That was shock. Shock is a feeling that is beyond communication, but you know when you have experienced it. I have seen many sex addicts experience this stage in my office as they discover the truth about their addiction.

Stage Two - Denial

I was in denial most of my life about my sex addiction. I always told myself things like "other people do this all the time" or "I'm special" to think this way. --Constance

To deny something means you have a "knowing" on some level that it is true. You can't deny something unless you know that there is some validity to it. So denial is a defense mechanism which allows you not to see, feel, or connect with the truth of what is real. For example, if someone died, we might say they are not dead. In this case, we would hope that denial would not last for a long time. Unfortunately in the case of addiction, denials can last for years, and in some situations can lead a person to death.

Denial is so great in sexual addiction it can kill. Sex addicts who are acting out in populations that are high risk for AIDS, simply say there is nothing wrong with it, and that they are not going to get AIDS. This is a defense mechanism which allows them to maintain their addiction.

Many sex addicts have numerous ways of denying their addiction before they come into an acceptance of being a sex addict. Some denial statements are "everybody does it," "I didn't lose my job," or "I'm not hurting anybody," "I'm still a good mom."

Denial is a way of saying "I'm not what I know I am." This can be contagious in a family system where everyone agrees that you are a wonderful person and so there is no one to confront your denial.

Denial is usually broken by two methods. One method is when the pain inside becomes so great that you experience the sincere reality that you are a sex addict. Another method can be experienced by getting threatened by divorce, or getting caught in an act of your addiction.

Denial is a phase that everyone goes through. The Twelve Steps help a recovering addict stay out of denial. Having people in your recovery group who love you enough to confront your denial is important. If you discover in your more rational moments that denial has been an issue for you, share this with your support team, such as your sponsor, group members, or spouse, so they can refresh your memory when your denial starts to sneak back in on you. Denial is tricky, and when you re-enter it, it will lead you to a path of destruction back into your addiction.

Some addicts have incurred serious consequences from going back into the addiction during denial. My encouragement is that if you are in denial about any part of your addiction, share what you are thinking with others who are serious about recovery. Believe behaviors rather than words.

Stage Three - Anger

I have processed through a lot of anger in my recovery. The last thing I wanted was to be a sex addict. I had given up alcohol years ago and swore I would never give up sex (a sex-addictive statement) --Constance

Anger is a good stage of grief. This means that you are finally interacting with the painful truth. You most likely don't like pain. It is uncomfortable and you may be mad. You may be mad that sometimes life has chosen to give you a limitation. You also may be mad that you can't act out the way you used to, or be with the people you were with in the past. You may be mad that a disease such as sex addiction is in your life. You could be mad that God has chosen to heal your sexual addiction. All of these things are a part of anger and grief. Being angry about the fact that some people can do something and you can't is normal and shows that you are making progress. It is not a sign that you are going backward. Eventually the anger will go away, or at least not be as prevalent, as you go through the various stages of grief. If you feel like there is a need to grapple with the anger, you can write your addiction a letter of what it has done to you over the years. This will help you work through your feelings. You can write about how your addiction has kept you from intimacy, honesty, enjoying life, and productivity. Anger will also come up if you are a survivor of abuse, which may have been a big factor in you becoming a sex addict. Anger shows that you are connecting with feelings.

If you find that you need further help with your anger, consult a therapist and discuss helpful techniques you can use to deal with your anger, so that you can move to the next stage. Anger is important to manage for you to maintain recovery.

Stage Four - Bargaining

I went through in my mind ways I could get involved in another relationship. Maybe I could start an affair no one in my recovery circle would know about. I was like a caged lion figuring out how I could get out. --Constance

Bargaining is a stage of grief that involves an "if...then" logic. For example, "If something wouldn't have been in my past, then I wouldn't have become a sex addict," or "If I could stop doing this for 30 days, I wouldn't be a sex addict." The bargaining can go on and on. It is an attempt to try to shift the pain and manipulate it to fit into categories, and still not experience the full impact of it. There is no shame in going through bargaining as long as you know that you are bargaining with your addiction.

If you are going to your Twelve Step meetings and keeping The Five Principles you are probably going to be okay. Allow some caring people to be aware of your statements and have them confront you when they hear them, so that you can continue to move into acceptance. Being who you are is the most freeing experience you will have. Your God-given limitations are there so that you can not destroy your life. Coming to that recognition is a part of grief. This is a normal process.

Stage Five - Sadness

I was surprised by the amount of sadness I felt. Sadness for how I treated others. Sadness for letting go of a coping mechanism. Sadness about being alone. --Constance

Sadness is going to come after you have been sober over a period of time and not just after attending meetings. When you start having feelings, one of the feelings you will experience is sadness. This sadness may be over the things lost because of your addiction, and because of the damage you may have caused and the risks that were taken. Some people think they are going into a depression when sadness does come. It can and it may effect you this way. Your eating, sleeping, and energy level may be disturbed. If this goes on for a long period of time, you will need to consult a therapist about it, but it is also normal to go through this stage. You will find some periods of crying unrelated to any significant event. You will feel vulnerable at times. You may find you are isolating yourself from others. It is sad that you have developed and behaved the way you did. And yet to recover, hope is just one more stage away. Experience the feeling of sadness, and understand that it is okay to feel this way because you are close to the end of your grief process. There is no way of getting through the grief process without feeling the emotion of sadness.

Stage Six - Acceptance

I'm coming to accept that I have this disease and I can no longer live like I use to. That I need to let go of old ideas about myself and others. That I can no longer use people for my selfish gratification. That I really need to grow, as painful as it is without relying on an addiction. --Constance

Acceptance is more than an intellectual or philosophical agreement that something is true. Acceptance is an integration that something is true. You can cognitively know that someone is dead, but integrating that and behaving as if it were true is a clear indicator that you have come to acceptance. In the case of sex addiction, you are behaving as if what you know to be true is true. You are going to meetings, making phone calls, have motivation toward recovery, and are finding creative solutions not to act out. It is an awareness that you are what God has created you to be, with a limitation in the area of sex, and you are willing to take responsibility for this. Part of revealing that you are in this stage of acceptance is behavioral. You need to behave as if you are a recovering sex addict and will find the greatest freedom in behaving as who you are, as opposed to trying to create an image or system to cover it up. In the acceptance stage, you will accept your sexual addiction and other painful events that have happened in your life.

Embracing Grief

Grief is something you will go through in various levels and at various times in your life, and so it is important that you look at how you grieve. One way to grieve is resistant. Resistant grief is when you push against the process. You don't want to feel the pain. You aren't praying and asking God to help you grieve or feel the pain. Consequently, the more you resist, the longer it is going to take. Grief has no agenda of its own. It doesn't necessarily take one or two years for each person. It is the disposition that you take with grief that determines how long it takes to go through the process. You can embrace grief and let it take you through the process of healing, or you can resist it and just let it stand by your side until you embrace it.

Embracing grief is coming to a place of knowing that recovery is a process, and that you are going through each of these stages of grief and embracing them. If you are reading this book, you are probably already out of shock and probably working toward moving out of denial and possibly even further. You are already to be congratulated, and yet there are more stages before you to go. The new life you will have of intimacy without secrets is just ahead of you, so continue to be encouraged. If you can embrace the process, you can expedite it to a certain degree.

Grief and Your Partner

Sex addicts are not the only ones, of course, who go through grief. Your addiction is not only a painful reality to you, but it is a painful reality to your partner and family. In looking at your partner, the grief process for them is a little different than the grief process for you. When you found out you were a sex addict and broke through your denial, you had a sense of relief (usually) that this is what you are. This is known as the "pink cloud syndrome" and it can last anywhere from four to six weeks, in which you feel so good that you have finally identified that you are a sex addict. During this time, you may not understand your partner's grief.

Your partner is experiencing some painful realities, such as you being a sexual addict, possible infidelity, or a risk of health. Your partner is going through a lot of pain. The loss of who he thought you were and who you actually are, is sometimes so diametrically opposed that he has to go through his grief to even begin to integrate all these realizations. When he finds out you're a sex addict, he is not going to go through a long stage of denial, although some may. More often than not, he already has known something has been wrong and begins to put together the pieces of times, events, and people.

He initially will spend most of his grief time in the anger stage. This anger can last anywhere from six weeks to six months. He will be mad at what he lost, because of the pretty picture that he thought he had of the both of you, or the feelings he had of knowing who you were and trusting you. I would encourage you to help him to get therapy. It is important for you to understand that his grief is real and this anger is not necessarily toward you as a person, but is towards your addiction. Depersonalizing this is going to be important, so that you don't attack back or do other things that are going to agitate his grief process. He will probably need to have his own therapy sessions about the addiction and behavior, so that he can be free to grieve appropriately. With some time and your hard work, he can go through the grief and healing he needs to experience. On the other side, you both have the hope of experiencing intimacy together.

Your husband or partner may find that recovery is difficult because he may think he needs to deal with this alone and not with the help of others. Feelings of inadequacy and failure can isolate him from reaching out for professional help or a support group.

A support group experience for him may be difficult as well, since he may think "he doesn't have a problem - you do." Also, most of the support groups for partners of sex addicts are predominantly women.

Some COSA and S-Anon groups have bought into the idea that men are sex addicts and men are the problem. He may need to go through an initial interview with the group to be able to attend. After the group feels he is appropriate, they will usually let him in the group. It is good for partner-support groups to see that this addiction is not just about men. He can heal, but he has to incorporate his own recovery. All you can do is encourage him and focus on your recovery.

Tips

Many of the women in our study offered suggestions that have worked for them in recovery that they thought may be helpful for you as well. I wanted to include these thoughts for beginning your recovery.

Be aware of feelings and feeling them. Live in the present. Be open and honest in all relationships. Go to at least three meetings a week. Work the 12 Steps. Say affirmations. Find and work with a sponsor. Practice 12 Step programs. Learn how to nurture yourself. Learn who you are, and what you like. Learn to say no and stand up for yourself. Read 12 Step literature and other literature related to this addiction. Continue to go to therapy and work on issues there, two times a month. Build a relationship with yourself and your Higher Power. Become more vulnerable to others.

Begin to buy clothes that help bring out the feminine side. Don't go shopping with the idea to buy something to seduce a man.

Necessary boundaries I put in place to stay clean: Not going out clubbing, dancing. No romantic or sexual stimulating reading, music, television, or movies. No surfing the internet personals. No looking for a man. Stop obsessive thoughts and fantasizing when I become aware of them . Abstinence from masturbation and learn about myself and my patterns. Make a connection with people in group and most important with my Higher Power. --Debra

I have had several counselors tell me to write letters to the people who I have hurt and have hurt me (never send them though) which has been helpful. Start journaling. I have much, much more to do. I have one day at a time to do that. --Julie

Don't go by or near certain types of places (i.e. bars), at least not alone - never go in. Come to honesty with pain issues. Learn to trust a few others and share, and get into previously unknown intimacy with God --Nancy

Avoid being alone with men. Call someone in recovery and "check in" with where you are physically, emotionally, spiritually, and process feelings (instead of stuffing, avoiding). Acknowledge feelings - name them (sad, frustrated), The 3 second rule is helpful (If fantasizing, focus on something else within 3 seconds). Wondering what to do about the people you acted out with (people you knew, only anonymous, etc.)? Talk about this and how you feel to your support group. --Constance

Take the first step to a therapist. --Francine

What to look out for in recovery: Accountability is the highest need in my recovery. Finding someone who is willing to understand what sexual addiction is and being willing to ask me accountable questions daily, such as how many men have I talked to? By phone? e-mail? chat room? personal contact? What plans am I considering? Do I consider myself "clean" today? --Wendy

One thing I have done is to put little signs on the inside of my front door so I can see them. One says, "Don't open the door!" That is to remind me not to even talk to the man out there. I know if I open the door, he will come in and we will have sex, eventually. The other sign says, "No, you can't come in! Go Away!" I can hold it up to the window so he can read it. I have trouble remembering to use the sign that says "go away", but I'm getting much better at just not opening the door. --Abby

The Twelve Steps

Now we enter into a recovery program known as the Twelve Steps. The original Twelve Steps were written many years ago for Alcoholics Anonymous. These alcoholics, after some period of sobriety, decided to write down the principles and the steps they took to maintain their sobriety and to live a healthier life. These principles and steps have been used throughout the world to help millions of people with various addictions, such as narcotic abuse, overeating, emotional problems, co-dependency, and sexual addiction.

The Twelve Steps of Alcoholics Anonymous: Adapted for Sexual Addicts

1. We admitted we were powerless over our sexual addiction, and that our lives had become unmanageable.

2. Came to believe that a power greater than ourselves could restore us to sanity.

3. Made a decision to turn our will and our lives over to the care of God, as we understood God.

4. Made a searching and fearless moral inventory of ourselves.

5. Admitted to God, to ourselves, and to another human being the exact nature of our wrongs.

6. Were entirely ready to have God remove all these defects of character.

7. Humbly asked God to remove our shortcomings.

8. Made a list of all persons we had harmed and became willing to make amends to them all.

9. Made direct amends to such people wherever possible, except when to do so would injure them or others.

10. Continued to take personal inventory, and when we were wrong, promptly admitted it.

11. Sought through prayer and meditation to improve our conscious contact with God as we understood God, praying only for knowledge of God's will for us and the power to carry that out.

12. Having had a spiritual awakening as the result of these steps, we tried to carry this message to others, and to practice these principles in all our day to day living.

Note: The Twelve Steps are reprinted and adapted with permission of Alcoholics Anonymous World Services, Inc. Permission to reprint and adapt the Twelve-Steps does not mean that AA has reviewed or approved the content of this publication, nor that AA agrees with the views expressed herein. AA is a program of recovery from alcoholism. Use of the Twelve Steps in connection with programs and activities which are patterned after AA, but which address other problems, does not imply otherwise.

In our study of women addicted to sex, we asked about Twelve Step group attendance. The following are the responses of the study.

In my recovery, I have attended a sex addiction or sex and love addiction support group.

67%   Yes
33%   No

In my recovery, I have attended a sex addiction, or love and sex addiction support group:

50%   as a regular part of my recovery.
25%   occasionally.
25%   not at all.

Constance shares with us her experience of Steps One through Four.

Step 1 - Step One is the most important step to me. I finally admitted to my inner most self that I was completely powerless over my sex addiction. When I no longer could control my obsessive thinking and craving of the body, I knew I was powerless and my life had become unmanageable.

Step 2 - At first I really didn't think I could be restored to sanity. As I started coming to the meetings and reading the SLAA book, I began to get some hope that I could recover. I had recovered from alcoholism by doing the steps so I knew they worked. I wasn't so sure they would work on this addiction, it seemed so powerful for an addiction. As I continued to share about the problem, a new hope arose and still leads me today.

Step 3 - I joined a step study which has helped immensely. I know my self-will and self-centerdness is at the root of my problem. I made the decision to turn my will and life over to God as I understood him. I had not completely turned this part of my life over to God in my previous experience with the steps.

Step 4 - I am currently working on this step in SLAA. This step is really helping me to face who I had become on self will. I am getting down to the root causes of my failure in life and relationships. I am

also becoming willing to make amends where I have done harm.
--Constance

A woman addicted to sex will benefit greatly by attending a Twelve Step support group. In light of this I felt it very important to have a dialogue and interpretation of these Twelve Steps.

An Interpretation of the Twelve Steps for Sex Addicts

In this section I will give my interpretation of the principles and concepts of the Twelve Steps as they are used for recovery from sexual addiction, so that you can implement them in your personal recovery. My comments here should not be construed as representing any particular Twelve Step fellowship. They are my own interpretation of the steps from many years of clinical experience helping sex addicts recover by using the Twelve Step process.

 We admitted we were powerless over our sexual addiction and that our lives had become umanageable.

We. I am so glad that the first word in the first step is "we." Sexual addiction is an international problem. "We" means that we have similar experiences and that we are alike. We grew up in the same family thousands of miles apart. We had the same kind of partners, sexual experiences, abuses, and neglects. "We" is a comforting word in this step. You can see that you are not alone and don't have to be alone. You can get better if you decide to get together. "We" is an encouraging word and is also essential. Without each other, we often fail to recover.

Admitted. This is a difficult word. Many of us have had situations in our childhood that we have had to admit. Maybe we stole something or something happened to us and we had to admit what we did. Do you remember those feelings of dread before admitting something? Then we went ahead and admitted it. We told what we did or what happened to us. After we admitted it, we felt less heavy or burdened, as if we could now move on. Admitting something for the woman addicted to sex is one of the hardest things to do in recovery. Admitting is a very important aspect of recovery and only those who admit to sexual addiction can move forward in recovery and life.

We Were Powerless. Again, I'm glad that there is a "we" in there and that I'm not the only one who is powerless. When we talk about power, we talk about control. Authority, strength, or force gives us the ability to be over someone else. But that is not what this word means. This word is powerless and as we know, the suffix "less" means without -- such as jobless.

This can be a tough reality for every addict. We are without any strength, power, control, or force to influence our addiction. This is why we need each other and a recovery program. Sometimes that is why we need therapy. We are powerless. We have tried alone to not sexually act out without success.

Our Sexual Addiction. The sexual addict is dependent on sex to deal with past pain and current stress. If sex is okay, then everything is okay, and as you know, there never is enough sex and we never really are okay. There seems to always be chaos and confusion. The female sex addict is someone whose soul is in pain. If it wasn't, she wouldn't have this addiction. Many sexual addicts, as mentioned earlier, have been sexually or emotionally abused. Many have additional addictions such as alcohol, drugs, or shopping. A female sex addict can be a complicated human being -- a human being in pain.

And That Our Lives. Our lives can be many things. It can be our physical, emotional, intellectual, or spiritual life. If you look at all the parts of our lives, they wouldn't equal the totality of our lives. Our lives are the very core of us. It is the inner part of us that identifies us as being separate from another person.

This is what has been affected as we look at our sexual addiction. This is the part that feels disconnected, alone, confused, and isolated when needs are not being met. It is this part of us that we are going to admit something very important about.

Had Become. These two words indicate to me that this has taken a while. It means that it took time, energy, process, and choices. It didn't just happen. It took a while and then eventually, it was made. Your life didn't become overwhelming or devastated instantly, but over a period of time.

Unmanageable. When we think about manageable, we think about things being in order or serene. We can tell when we walk into a store whether the store is manageable or unmanageable. This word means unorganized and chaotic. If someone came from the outside and saw this, they would say "What a mess!" Sometimes this is the way we feel about our lives, and our feelings can be valid. Our lives in many of the areas we have talked about have become unmanageable, unconnected, uncontrollable, and unpredictable. No matter how hard we have tried to make them look good or perfect, they don't and they are not. Our lives have become empty and hollow in many respects. Now, through Step One, if we can admit this unmanageability, we have a strong hope of recovery.

I encourage everyone to take Step One seriously because it is the foundation of the Twelve Step program. It will cause you to have a good house of recovery to live in for the future.

 Came to believe that a power greater than ourselves could restore us to sanity.

Came to Believe. Again, notice the step is written in the past tense. The original steps were written to share the process that the original members of AA went through in recovery. There was a process through which they came to believe.

It is really a simple process. You come to believe many things during your lifetime. For example, you came to believe that there was a Santa Claus. Later you came to believe that there wasn't a Santa Claus. As you grew older, you may have come to believe that a certain person liked you, and later realized they didn't like you. We come to believe certain religious and political positions. There is some consistency to this process throughout our lives. In this process, there is a definite point at which you understand or come to believe.

In Twelve Step groups, the process of coming to believe is something that often happens as a result of exposure to other recovering people. You may not necessarily know the date or the hour when you did come to believe, but you know that you feel differently, and you begin to have hope. This is so important in recovery, because knowing that you have come to believe, or knowing you do believe, can save your life. Women addicted to sex can feel hopeless or worthless, experience severe shame and guilt from past traumas or present circumstances, and resort to sad behaviors or destruction, isolation, sexual acting out, and suicidal ideation. If you have come to believe, you have hope.

A Power. "A" is a common word. You use it everyday. A cat, a dog, a book -- and in every context in which it is used, it denotes one. If you were going to use a word to describe more than one, you would say "these," or another word that indicates plurality. This step is not written in the plural. It says "a" power greater than ourselves. This is significant. Being an "a" here, you realize that there is one entity, one strength, one energy, one spirit, one power. It is significant that as you come to believe, you are believing in one.

Greater Than Ourselves. This is one of the first areas which requires trust. We now know that there is one that is greater than ourselves. This is the best news we have in recovery, that we don't have to figure this out alone. As you begin to trust this power, you begin to recover from the sick patterns, poor choices, and undesirable relationships that have been a big part of your past.

In the original context of AA, this power greater than ourselves indicated that the power was greater than that first group of recovering alcoholics. This one single power was greater than a whole group. That's a lot of power. People in recovery frequently first recognize this power in the group, but in reality it is greater than the group. Even if you had a power greater than yourself, you may have had difficulty accessing the resources of that power and applying them to your life. In the program, you believe this power has more ability to solve life's problems than you do individually. What a relief!

Could. "Could" is one of the most, loving expressions in the Twelve Steps. "Could" means that this power has the ability, the resources, the energy, the intention of helping you along in the recovery process? It is possible now to begin to be restored. It is possible now to begin to be healthy, to have loving relationships with loving people, to be loved and nurtured in a healthy way. It can be done, and this power can do it. It is the experience of many in sexual addiction recovery that, if given the freedom and the opportunity -- in other words, if you quit trying to do it all on your own -- this power will do for you what you have been unable or unwilling to do for yourself. All you have to do is ask.

Restore Us to Sanity. "Restore" means bringing something back. Frequently when you think of restoration, you may think of restoring an automobile or an old house, and making it look like new. The same is true of sexual addiction recovery. Women addicted to sex have for so long been robbed of spirituality, intimacy, trust, and even their own reality. In a world that should have been safe, they have been violated again and again with secrets.

Insanity is natural when you live with a disease as crazy as sexual addiction. You may have difficulty applying the idea of insanity to yourself, but often having two life-styles at the same time and living with secrets can make most women addicted to sex feel insane. You try again and again to do something that should work, but doesn't. You try and try to fix the problems that sexual addiction creates in your life without success.

The behaviors themselves are insane, but the fact that you use them again and again, never stopping to realize that they're not working, qualifies you to be restored to sanity. It is possible for female sex addicts to be restored to sanity. Those already in recovery have experienced it. They are living proof that it is possible to make better choices, and we hope, as you read this, you know that it is possible for you. You may still feel crazy, but if you have gotten this far in your recovery, you have a good chance at finding sanity.

 Made a decision to turn our wills and our lives over to the care of God, as we understood God.

Made. The word "Made" is similar to the word "became." It indicates a process which involves time and choices, but there is definitely a time designated when it is done. For example, when a child in school makes an ashtray in art, or a meal or dress in home economics, there is a time when it is in the process of being made, and then it is completed. It is made. "Made" is something that has been coming along, but is finally resolved to the point that you can say it is done.

A. Here again we come to that little word, "a." It is one. What we are discussing in Step Three is a one time event. Many people want to spread this step out, but as you move along in this process of working the steps, you will see why we only make this decision one time.

Decision. When you make a decision, you list the good and the bad, the pros and cons of a situation. In this step, you can make a list of what you have done with your life in the past, and how you could deal with your life differently in the future. Such a list makes it easier to make the decision you are asked to make in Step Three. It is a decision.

Compare it to a traditional courtship and marriage. It is like you had an engagement period in Step Two, during which you get to know your Power greater than yourself, and you began to get comfortable with the idea of having God in your life. Step Three is the marriage ceremony itself, where you make a commitment to share your life with God. You just have a single ceremony, but it sets the stage for further development through the relationship. Step Three asks you to be willing to share your life with God. The decision is a one time event, but it provides a means for further growth.

To Turn. Turning can be expressed in many ways. Someone once said that turning means "to flip over," kind of like a hot cake. The hot cake gets done on one side, and then you have to turn it over.

It is a pretty simple definition of "Turn," but it is also pretty profound. If you flip over, you make a total change from the way you have been up to this point.

The word "Turn" is used on highways all over the world to indicate direction: signs may indicate a left or right turn, or U-turn. When you make a U-turn, you turn around and go in the opposite direction. What you do in Step Three is definitely a U-turn! You turn away from your limited understanding of how life should be. You leave behind perceptions, experiences, and ideas about things you thought you understood. You turn from them and gain a whole new perspective. This is an essential part of recovery. You are turning into something, or turning somewhere else, and it is amazing how far that turn can take you, as you continue in your recovery efforts.

Our Will. Again, this is plural, as the group stays and works together. In this group of safe people, who have turned their wills and lives over to God, you will begin to see this decision as a possibility for yourself. But what is your will? The simplest definition of "Will" is probably the ability to make the choices you do for your life. In the group, you will begin to turn over the choices that you make to God. This can be an easy thing for some, but for others it can be a very hard thing to do. It means you must turn your choices over to God, try to understand God's perspective, and follow that perspective in your life. That is why Step Three is so powerful.

As I have mentioned before, in many recovery groups there is a phrase called "stinking thinking." Stinking thinking is the way an addict, alcoholic, or a non-recovering person thinks. This thinking doesn't work. The choices non-recovering people make don't bring about positive results. There seems to be a certain self-destructiveness to their choices and behavior. Step Three cuts to the core of stinking thinking. It is the beginning of a new life-style.

Giving up their wills is a safety valve for sex addicts. In making decisions about relationships, they are now able to turn to God. As they do, God will demonstrate new directions they can take, and new choices they can make. They will begin getting answers, and will be able to make different choices about their sexual behavior. This is a freedom that is only gained by letting go of their own will, or choices.

Our Lives. Our lives are the result of all our choices. For each individual, life is the totality of all parts. When you turn it all over -- spiritually, emotionally, physically, socially, financially, and sexually -- you give yourself to God. You begin to trust God. You begin to believe that God will take care of you.

You may say this is frightening: "How can I trust God?!" But simply look at what you have trusted in the past. You have trusted your own ability to think, and your own ability to make choices. You have taken the advice of a few chosen people who have not necessarily acted in your best interest.

Turning your will and life over is necessary. It is through this trust experience with God that you begin to believe that God loves you. You begin once again to trust yourself. Eventually, you can even regain your trust in people. Step Three is an essential part of working the steps. It is not a luxury. It is necessary for a healthy, happy life. Working the steps is not always easy, and often you do not understand why you must work them. Often the steps are understood only after they have been completed. Then you realize the beauty of this spiritual process, and open yourself to further growth and joy, as you walk this road with others who are making the same steps toward recovery.

The Care of God. What do you think of when you hear the word "Care?" It is often expressed in terms of someone who loves you, someone who demonstrates some kindness toward you, someone who is willing to get involved in your life, willing to get in there and be patient with you to work with you, and not condemn you in the process; someone who can be nurturing. All these pictures of a loving friend can represent care. Care is felt in the release of energy from one person to another, usually through kind behaviors, like providing a listening ear or some other sign of concern.

How does this relate to God? What is the care of God? It is simply God's willingness to be involved in a nurturing, supportive, accepting way in your life. God is concerned for women addicted to sex. God's concern for others in this world demonstrates that care. You can sometimes see it more clearly in the lives of others than you can in your own life. For some female sex addicts, the group is a manifestation of the care of God in their lives. It is possible for you, by looking at others in your support group, to connect with this issue in such a way that it radically changes your life. Something as simple as their support can be seen as the extension of God's care and concern.

Now, we'll talk about God. The original writers of the Twelve Steps changed only one word from the initial version. In Step Two they changed the word "God." to "a Power greater than ourselves." That is the only change they made, and it was made for this reason: Those first alcoholics said that God was too scary for the recovering person in Step Two. Maybe the recovering person had too many hurts, too many problems with God, so the word was changed to "a Power greater than ourselves" to give the newcomer an engagement period, and allow them to experience God through the group's care, nurturing, and love. In this way, they could come to believe in a caring God who could, and would, help them.

But who is God? Let me share my thoughts with you on this subject. Simply put, God is Love. God is also in authority, or in control, especially for those who turn their lives and will over to Him, switching the authority from themselves to God.

According to what you have learned so far in the steps, God has the ability to restore you. God is more powerful than you are alone, or in a group. God is one who gets actively involved in your life, who has more power and more success than you in dealing with sexual addiction. This God can and will help you as you work the Twelve Steps.

For many, this understanding of God will develop into a faith that is common in the American culture, and will enable the recovering female sex addict to enjoy the benefits of finding a community that shares the same faith as she does. Some will not. It is a universal blessing of this program, if they are willing, to come to a greater relationship with God, as they understand God.

The people who have turned their wills and lives over to the care of a God they understand -- who have turned their choices over to God -- often have more understanding of how God works and how God thinks. The group is a good resource, especially for those early in recovery who want an understanding of God. It is very important to realize, as it pertains to understanding God, that no single person is going to understand the totality of God, but the members of your support group can be helpful in this journey.

As We Understood God. One way to interpret this is to compare your understanding of God with the way you function in relationships with people, because we are talking about a relationship. When you first meet someone, your knowledge of them is limited. Only through time, communication, and commitment to any relationship do you really come to understand another person. The same is true in your relationship with God. Coming to understand God is a process which is available to any and all in recovery, who are willing to turn their wills and lives over, so that they can experience a new life, a new freedom, and find happiness. The beauty of finding God in the Twelve Steps is that as you grow, your understanding of God grows too.

 *Made a searching and fearless moral inventory of ourselves.*

Made A Searching. Searching holds the possibility of fun, but for female sex addicts, searching can be extremely painful. When you search, you intend to find something. For example, when you lose your keys, you go searching, with the intent of finding the keys. As you begin your inventory, you are searching, you are scrutinizing, you are seeking with intent to find something that is quite significant.

In this context, "Searching" indicates that you will have to expend some energy. This is the beginning of what is often referred to in the program as the "action steps." You now begin to take action in your own behalf. Note that this step is also in the past tense. As you begin your inventory, you can know that others have passed this way before, and have survived and gotten better. You are not alone.

Fearless. "Fearless" simply means without fear. This is the attitude with which you approach your moral inventory. Being fearless allows you to view your inventory objectively, as you uncover the pain. You will be looking at what was done to you, and what you have done to yourself and others.

Many of the experiences you will be looking at are extremely painful. For some, the painful experience was childhood sexual abuse; for others, it was forced oral sex or rape. For some, it will be something they would much rather not even remember, something they may think they only imagined. Fearlessness will lead you to look at your own part in the sick relationships you have been in as an adult, and at the patterns that have been repeated over and over in your life. You need to look at these things with an attitude of courage and bravery. You can, because in Step Three you turned your will and life over to the care of a loving God.

Moral. "Moral" can be defined as right and wrong, categories of black and white, or good and bad. Something that is immoral could be defined as something that violates your conscience. As you look at your life in Step Four, you will be looking for things that you've done that have violated your conscience. For example, as children, many of us had the experience of raiding the cookie jar. We knew that we were not supposed to get a cookie. There might not be anything wrong with having a cookie, but we were told not to, so it became wrong. Yet we waited until our parents could not see, and took a cookie anyway. It probably tasted good, but we may have felt badly afterward. We felt badly because we knew we did something wrong.

In Step Four, you will also be looking at how you were violated by others. Have you ever said to yourself, "If they really knew me, they wouldn't like me. If they knew I was sexually abused or raped, they wouldn't be my friend." The shame and guilt you carry from the actions of other people toward you can be overwhelming. Step Four is designed to release you from that shame and guilt, as you look at how your moral code has been violated by others.

It is wrong to believe that you are unworthy because of your past. In recovery, you come to know yourself and let others know you. Step Four is about coming to know yourself, being honest with yourself about what happened, taking into account how it affected your life, and where it leaves you today.

In short, Step Four is an inventory. You will list everything that happened, even if it involved others and you were simply an innocent bystander -- as in the case of the divorce of parents, or the death of a grandparent, or other significant family member. Such an event may not have had anything to do with your morals, but it did affect you emotionally.

Inventory. What are you to inventory in Step Four? You inventory your experiences because, that is what you have on hand. You inventory your memory, for that is what you have been given to record your experiences. Many see this inventory as a life story. It is a process where you begin to see the truth of what you've done, and what has been done to you. Some things will be negative; others will be positive. When a storekeeper takes inventory, he lists not only the things he wants to get rid of, but the things he wants to keep. And he doesn't just make a mental note of it -- he writes it down.

Step Four is a written assignment. You will need to have pen or pencil, paper, and a quiet place where you can be uninterrupted. Some just begin writing. Some or ganize their inventory by ages, such as one to six years, seven to twelve years, and so on. Still others have done it by first listing all the traumatic events they can remember -- things that were done to them or by them that violated their value system -- and then writing how they felt at the time, and how they feel now about those events. There is no right or wrong way to write an inventory. The important thing is just to do it. You will be face to face for perhaps the first time with the total reality of your life. It can be pretty overwhelming, so don't be afraid to let your sponsor or therapist know how you are feeling while writing your inventory. As you transfer your story to paper, you are also transferring the pain, guilt, and shame onto paper. Writing an inventory can be a very positive, transforming experience, and it is also quite vital to your recovery.

Of Ourselves. Once again, you can see this is plural. You can know that others have done this before. You can and will survive the pain of writing your inventory down. It is joyous to see others freed from their shame. As you see other members of your support group complete their inventories, you will begin to believe that this release from past shame can happen for you too. You are reminded that only you can do this for yourself. Only you know your pain, the strength of your fears, and your deepest secrets. Only you are qualified to write this inventory. Now is the time to decide for yourself who you are, and who you want to be. There is great freedom in taking your focus off what is wrong with others, and doing a searching and fearless moral inventory of yourself. You may not understand the value of this step until you have completed it, but it is well worth the pain and tears to move past the secret and further down the road to a successful recovery.

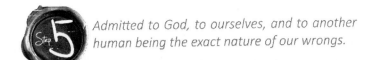

Admitted to God, to ourselves, and to another human being the exact nature of our wrongs.

Admitted. Here you are again, looking at that word, "Admitted." You already know that it means to "fess up," or acknowledge what is already true. You may have already experienced the pain and joy of doing this, probably as a child or adolescent. Perhaps you put yourself in a situation you knew your parents would not approve, or did something wrong, and knew you were going to have to tell them, because you knew they were going to find out anyway. Do you remember your feelings of guilt and shame, like you had let yourself and them down? Then you somehow got the courage to tell them what you had done. You admitted the truth -- no matter the consequences. It felt better, finally, to let the secret out.

The same is true in Step Five. You admit all that you have written in your Fourth Step. You let out all those secrets, and finally feel that clean joy which comes from truly being totally known.

To God. God might be the easiest person to tell, or the hardest, depending on your relationship with Him. If you feel God has let you down before, admitting what has been wrong in your life can be particularly difficult. Fortunately, God is forgiving of all that you have done, and is willing to restore any lost part of yourself. As one wise person in recovery stated, "It's okay to tell God. God already knows it all anyway, and is just waiting for us to be honest about it too."

To Ourselves. Admitting your past secrets to yourself often takes place as you write your Fourth Step, if you are truly fearless and thorough when writing it. Admitting your powerlessness, your need to be restored to sanity, your profound amazement at your poor choices, and your sincere sense of having failed yourself is probably the most humbling experience you will have with regard to your sense of who you are.

It is at this point, though, that the recovery of your true self is able to take an upward turn, without the overwhelming sense of shame or guilt that has been so closely bound to you in the past. You are now able to begin a more shame-free life, which empowers you to experience the next and most essential part of this step: being able to reveal yourself to another human being.

And to Another Human Being. "What? I have to tell all this stuff to somebody else, face to face?" Yes, telling your story to another human being is one of the most crucial parts of your recovery. In writing your Fourth Step, you have taken your total history of shame, hurt, abandonment, abuse, and poor choices of acting out, and poured it consciously into one place. Your Fourth Step may even have brought to your conscious awareness some things you have been suppressing for years, and now all of these memories are in one place. If all this pain is kept inside you, and is not shared with another human being, you may talk yourself into believing once again that you are unlovable or unacceptable with such a painful, messy past. You could use this negative information and history for condemnation instead of healing. That is why we must tell another person. We must realize that we are loved and accepted even though we have been places and experienced things of which we are not proud.

In this Fifth Step you experience spiritually, emotionally, and often physically, a cleansing or a lightening of your load. As you share who you have been and what you have experienced with another trusted person, you are reassured that nothing you have done makes you unlovable. Now someone knows the whole truth, and still loves you. It is remarkable!

A note of caution is appropriate here: When you choose someone to hear your Fifth Step, it is important to pick the least condemning, most loving and accepting woman you know. You might choose a therapist, sponsor, or spiritual person you trust. Choose someone who understands that you are digging into your past in order to make your present, and future better -- someone who will not shame you for your past. This person can be a member of your support group as well. This choice is yours. Make it in your best interest.

The Exact Nature of Our Wrongs. The fact that this part of the step is so specific will help two kinds of people: those who say, "I can't be specific so I'll never really feel loved," and those who believe that they can own everybody else's wrongs and avoid looking at their own choices. The first person needs to be specific in sharing her story, because the shame she experiences about the past, is tied to specific episodes. We must talk about those specific episodes to relieve the shame associated with them. The second person needs to acknowledge her own shortcomings and "clean her own side of the street" -- not anyone else's -- so that she too can be freed from her own shame.

It's a recognized fact that you can't free anyone else from their shame. Each person has to work their own program of recovery, in order to have the kind of happy and fulfilling life we are all capable of experiencing. As a note of caution, for those who have violated children, most states demand professionals report it if the specific name and place of this event is given to them. In sharing this information be aware of this when doing your Fifth Step.

 Were entirely ready to have God remove all these defects of character.

Were Entirely Ready. As you move from Step One through Step Five, you will discover a process through which you recognize powerlessness, find a God of your understanding, go inside yourself by writing an inventory, and let someone else know who you really are. The very core of the program is in the first five steps. By working these steps you have learned to "trust God and clean house."

Now that you have cleaned house, you must learn how to maintain your new surroundings. It is one process to clean a dirty house, whether you got it dirty yourself or just inherited all the mess -- and it is another thing entirely to make sure that it never gets dirty again. That is what Step Six and the following steps are all about -- preventative maintenance.

You start by being "Entirely Ready." This simply means that you are 100 percent ready to look at the damage that was done by all that trash, and you evaluate what you can throw away. You might be quite attached to some of that stuff. Even though it doesn't work any longer, you hesitate to give it up. Someday, some of those old behaviors might come in handy, you keep thinking. You forget that each time you try on old behavior it causes great pain. "Were Entirely Ready" indicates that you are finally tired of the pain. You finally realize that changing is not quite as frightening as staying the same.

To Have God. Having God in our lives is so significant for the woman addicted to sex. Here in Step Six they are reminded that they, like everyone, are blessed by having a relationship with God. They are beginning to believe that God does want the best for them, and that God wants their lives to express this new way of feeling and believing about themselves. God is willing to work with you, as you continue your efforts at recovery.

Remove All. This sounds like an unrealistic, maybe even painful statement, at least from a human standpoint. "Remove" indicates loss. Female sex addicts have certainly experienced loss in their lives. But to lose, or remove, all of their defects? How?

Well, it isn't up to you to decide how, it's only up to you to be ready. Remember that earlier you recognized that you don't have a whole lot of power of your own. In Step Six you will rely on God to have the power to change you -- the power you've been unable to access in your addiction.

Defects Of Character. As you consider the term, "defects of character," you might be thinking of some of the ways you have behaved. Go ahead and get a pencil and paper, and write down what comes to mind. Reviewing your inventory should give you a good idea of things about your character you might want changed. For example, perhaps the way you express your anger indicates a defect of character. Maybe the way you control, and try to manipulate your spouse or children, or the way you pout to get your own way, or isolate or run away from responsibility for yourself, are things you want to change. Honesty is important in listing these defects, because the ones you hold on to will keep you stuck in old patterns, and you will continue to attract unhealthy people into your life, especially in intimate relationships.

It is the experience of many recovering sex addicts that as they become more healthy and honest themselves, they gravitate toward more healthy, honest people, and are better able to determine who is unhealthy. Understanding this can certainly motivate you to really look at your defects of character, and be 100 percent willing to have God remove them. This helps prevent the dust and trash from resettling in your house.

 Humbly asked God to remove our shortcomings.

Humbly. Many struggle with the word, "Humble," having been humiliated time and again by sexual addiction. Humility is not the same as humiliation, although you may feel something like humiliation as you see the devastation in your own life, and the lives of those around you caused by your defects of character. Humility, in this case, means recognizing your true humanness. You see in Step Seven the manner with which you should approach God. Humility means knowing that you don't have the power to change yourself, but that God does. You come into God's presence with a humble heart, but with hope as well. And as you ask, you shall receive. As long as you don't have preconceived ideas of just how and when God will remove your defects of character, you will have them removed.

Asked God. Humility requires that we ask, not tell, God anything. By now perhaps you have come to believe that God really does want the best for you; wants you to be free of your defects of character; wants you to feel good about yourself, and to be attracted to healthy people. You are asking, in a sense, to do God's will.

To Remove Our Shortcomings. In Step Six you became ready. Now you push the "Go" button, and ask God to take your defects of character, or shortcomings. It would be nice if it happened all at once, but again you will experience it as a process. In this process, God will be with you throughout your life, removing your shortcomings as you continue to identify them when they surface, as long as you are willing to ask for help.

For some addicts, this step comes easily. For others, it is very hard, especially if they are holding on, still rationalizing, still defending, still gripping your defense mechanisms. In that case, Step Seven can be a painful experience. As someone once said in a meeting, "There was never anything I let go of that didn't have claw marks all over it, including my defects of character."

You can trust that if you ask, God will remove your defects of character, no matter how much you resist. If you decide to hold on to them, you will be fighting a losing battle. It is at this point that you will really need your support group. They will give you valuable feedback about any shortcomings they see you holding on to. If you aren't sure, ask questions. They will also give you support as you try new behaviors in place of the old ones that kept you so unhappy. Allow them to support you in this growth process.

 Made a list of all persons we had harmed, and became willing to make amends to them all.

Made A List. You probably don't have any problem shopping for groceries if you've made a list. You know that the most efficient way to shop is to have a written list, instead of just mental notes, because otherwise you are likely to get home and find you have forgotten some essential items. There is a saying in Alcoholics Anonymous that you should be fearless and thorough from the very start. This is true in Step Eight. Again, take a pencil and paper in hand, and looking at your inventory, make a list of all those you have harmed. This list should include yourself as well as others, and can also include what damage was done, and the person's name.

Of All Persons. Here again is that sometimes scary word: "All." "All" means every single one. You are, once again, being challenged to be honest. To the degree that you can be honest in making this list, you will have hope for new relationships with important people in your life.

We Had Harmed. It takes an honest person to look at their life and see the people they have harmed. It is often easier to see how you have been harmed by others. In Steps Four and Five, you looked at how you have been hurt by trusted people in your life; how you have been traumatized; how you have been emotionally abandoned; and how you have suffered. But if all you look at is how you have been harmed, you are only halfway healed.

Just as it can be painful for a recovering alcoholic to see how her drinking damaged those around her, so it can be painful for the recovering sex addict to realize what she has done to hurt others. For many female sex addicts, it is much more comfortable to be the victim. As a matter of fact, they have often been the victim of their own behavior, from their past and even recent relationships. But past victimization by others just makes it that much more difficult for these people to realize that they have actually harmed other people. The acting-out behavior is just the start of this list. The harm can be very subtle. You need to really search your mind and heart, in order to complete your healing.

And Became Willing. The past tense here reminds you, one more time, that the hard work demanded in the previous steps is survivable. Female sex addicts have worked their way through these steps before, and have found peace and happiness on the other side. It also indicates a process. Recovery doesn't just happen overnight.

Becoming willing takes time for everyone, especially if they are holding onto a victim status.

To Make Amends. What does it mean to "Make Amends?" For sex addicts, or anyone in recovery for that matter, to make amends means to acknowledge the wrong they have done, and be willing to be different. You stop blaming the other person to justify your own behavior. You stop rationalizing, and defending yourself. You stop avoiding responsibility. You are continuing to change in your relationships with yourself and others. You take full responsibility for what you have done, and to whom you have done it, at least on paper at this point.

To Them All. Here is that word "All" again. It seems to appear everywhere throughout the steps. By now, your list should include everyone who has in any way been harmed by your actions or lack of actions. You should have found the willingness to be different with each person on that list, including yourself. No stone should be left unturned at this point, or you will still carry old guilt that will keep you stuck in old, sick patterns of thinking and relating. With names, phone numbers, and accounts of damages in hand, you are ready to move on.

 Made direct amends to such people wherever possible, except when to do so would injure them or others.

Made Direct Amends. In Step Eight, you made your list. In Step Nine, you actually go to the people on your list and make direct amends to them for the inappropriate attitudes or behaviors you have had in the past that have affected them. Notice again that this step is written in the past tense. These steps were written in the late 1930s when the first members of Alcoholics Anonymous became sober. Working these steps, especially Step Nine, was something they had to do to maintain their sobriety, so they would not have to carry the pain, shame, or guilt of the past, or present, into their new sober lives.

They had to be honest with themselves. So do you as you go to each person on your list and ask them for their forgiveness. When you acknowledge how your behavior affected your relationships with them, you will find the most incredible freedom. Tremendous emotional weights can be lifted, and often relationships can be restored, as the result of working Step Nine. This is not a 100 percent guarantee, since some relationships will remain fractured. However, at least your side of the street will be clean.

You will begin to feel wholeness and happiness in your life, now that you have made the effort to vent completely, without expectations. This is a significant point You do not make amends with the expectation that your friends, or family will change their behavior. You do not make amends with the expectation that people will respond in any certain way. People may, in fact, respond when you make amends, but it is by no means the motivation for you to do what you must to get rid of what you have been carrying for so long. Inflated expectations can cause you much pain, because others are not always in the same place with their recovery that you are with yours. Many people do not choose a path of recovery at all. Your personal efforts and behavior however, can challenge them into this kind of recovery at some point in their future.

It is not a given that the other person will ask forgiveness in return, even though they may have injured you much more than you have injured them. Your goal is to clean your own slate. You are not responsible for what others leave undone, nor can their shortcomings keep you from recovering and feeling good about yourself.

Except When To Do So Would Injure Them or Others. When you get to this point, you may become confused when you attempt to decide if making amends will injure the person involved, or be detrimental to others, possibly innocent people. Such confusion is best resolved with the assistance of a group, sponsor, or therapist. Confusion is not to be used; however, as an excuse to not make any amends because you don't want to experience the pain or shame of admitting your past behavior.

What you must consider, when admitting past behavior, is whether or not your confession would so significantly damage the other person involved that you should not raise the issue to them. You can ask yourself, "Would this be damaging?" If you have a question, do not assume you have the answer. You could very possibly avoid an amend which could restore a relationship, or hold on to an amend that will set you up for old behavior. Go over your list with a sponsor, support group or therapist if at all possible BEFORE YOU START YOUR STEP NINE!

 Continued to take personal inventory and when we were wrong, promptly admitted it.

Continued. Here again you must deal with the maintenance of your newly clean house. You are not letting the dust fall. You are not letting the dirt collect, or the garbage overflow in the can. Here you are in a process, as in Steps Four and Five. Today, when you have been inappropriate or have violated anyone's boundaries, including your own, you don't have to wait five or ten years to make amends. You can do it as you go along.

To Take Personal Inventory. Taking a daily personal inventory is a process in which female sex addicts are able to look at each person in their life, and see how they are interacting with this person. They look at their attitudes toward others and honestly evaluate them. This is not done to the point where they are unable to enjoy interactions, but it is an honest evaluation of how they respond to peers, family, and in all other relationships. It also is a reminder that you inventory only your own behavior, not anyone else's.

And When We Were Wrong, Promptly Admitted It. You will be wrong. This part of Step Ten says, "When," not, "If," you were wrong. Many sex addicts have been wronged, but there will still be times when you will be wrong yourself. It is so important for the recovering person to stay free, and not enter into a place of guilt and shame, which can push you into some acting-out behavior. So, in the maintenance of Step Ten, when you are wrong, you promptly admit it. "Promptly" is significant because it keeps you from holding on to the baggage, thinking for months about whether you were or weren't wrong. Promptly means admit it right now, right here. If you have been acting inappropriately, say, "I'm sorry. Forgive me, I'm acting inappropriately." It is as simple as that. Step Ten gives you a way to stay free from the bondage of guilt and shame. It keeps you humble, which often helps you to remain healthy.

Sought through prayer and meditation to improve our conscious contact with God as we understood God, praying only for knowledge of God's will for us and the power to carry that out.

Sought Through Prayer and Meditation. This step not only tells you what you are doing, but it also tells you how to do it. You are seeking. You are looking to improve your relationship with God. This step tells you to do that through prayer and meditation. Prayer is that verbal and sometimes internal communication with God. It is such a positive experience for the woman who is a sex addict to become more aware of God in her life. This step lets you know that it is your responsibility. Seeking requires action on your part. You may have felt abandoned by God, since you put no real effort into trying to find out where He was. It has been said many times in meetings, "If you can't find God, guess who moved." You move away from God, God never moves away from you. Seeking Him is all that it takes to find Him.

Meditation is sometimes a deeper sense of prayer. Prayer is requesting, asking, interacting. Meditation is listening and hearing God's voice. A lot of humans experience rest and peace through meditation, and are able to still the constant obsessive thinking that prevents them from hearing what God has to say: that they are significant, they are loved, and they deserve to be healthy.

Meditate on God's character, on your personal relationship with Him, on some scripture or recovery material you have, and allow them to really sink into your spirit. Be still and God will speak to you.

To Improve Our Conscious Contact With God. Most women addicted to sex, like many people, have an unconscious contact with God. They rely most of the time on their own thinking and resources, and connect with God only after they have thoroughly botched their lives. Step Eleven reminds you to keep God in your conscious mind. You are then able to experience the power and love of God in a whole new way. As a result, you will experience life in a whole new way. You will have a higher sense of purpose and joy. The result of this new awareness of God on a moment-to-moment basis is a better relationship with God. As with any relationship, efforts at improving the relationship require time, energy, and some sort of communication. With time you will find the method of communication that works best for you. There is no right or wrong way to do it.

As We Understood God. It is impossible for any one of us to totally understand God. Indeed, my understanding of God might not work for you, nor yours for me. The beauty of the program is that you can begin to see evidence of God in other people. Remember this is not a job you undertake on your own. You come to a new understanding of God as you interact with the people in your support group, church, or other community of people seeking knowledge of God. As you listen, you will grow in understanding through other people's experiences of God in their lives.

Praying Only For Knowledge of God's Will For Us. By now you are beginning to see the benefits of letting go of self will. In Step Eleven, you are gently reminded that when you pray for God's will in your life, you are asking for the absolute best solution to whatever you are facing. So often we push and push situations to turn out the way we want them to, only to find out that we got second or third, or seventh, or tenth best. It is a very positive thing to realize that you can trust God to have your best interests at heart. The people, places and things you have given your will over to in the past did not have your best interests at heart. You now trust God enough to say, "Not my will, but Thy will be done."

And The Power to Carry That Out. You pray for knowledge of God's will, not just for the sake of having the information, but also for the power to carry it out.

Having the information without the willingness or power to carry it out, will not change anything. After prayer for the knowledge, you can now listen in meditation for God to tell you the things you need to do. Sometimes a path will open, sometimes God will bring to mind a defect of character that is getting in your way, and sometimes God will challenge you in the way you are behaving through intuitive thoughts or feelings you may have. Often the power to make the changes God seems to want you to make comes through the people in your support groups. It can even come from seeing someone stuck in old behaviors. You can be motivated to change by seeing the consequences others are experiencing because of their unwillingness to act differently. Once having asked for direction and listened for guidance, you can act with assurance, knowing that if you are on the wrong track, you will come to know it. And you always know that you're not alone.

 Having had a spiritual awakening as the result of these steps, we tried to carry this message to others and to practice these principles in all our day-to-day living.

Having Had A Spiritual Awakening As The Result Of These Steps. It is no wonder that a woman who comes to the steps -- and in the process of time admits to powerlessness, admits to humanness, the need for a relationship with God, actively pursues that relationship, cleans house, makes amends, and maintains this behavior -- has a spiritual awakening. This spiritual awakening is the purpose of working the steps. It is an awakening in which the woman who is addicted to sex discovers that she does have worth and value, that she is loved by God, and can be loved by others, if she will only believe in her lovableness and open up her heart and let that love in.

The awakening to a spiritual connection with God can give the female addict the power to change her ways of relating to herself and the world. She can now see herself as a precious child of a loving God, and treat herself and others accordingly.

We Tried to Carry This Message to Others. In the beginning of Alcoholics Anonymous, it was not a matter of a drunk alcoholic seeking advice and support from someone who was sober. It was the recovering alcoholic who sought out the active drinker. Bill W., the co-founder of AA, knew that if he couldn't share what he had discovered about his relationship with God and its importance to his sobriety, he wouldn't be able to stay sober. This is true for sex addicts too. As you progress in your recovery, and become less absorbed in your own pain, you begin to recognize when others around you are in pain. You will begin to see opportunities to share your experience, strength, and hope with other sex addicts who are suffering from the same low self esteem, dependency, or independency problems, and lack of boundaries that you experienced. And you will share, not to get them well, but to remain mindful of the miracle of recovery in your own life. Without constant reminders, you are likely to forget where your strength and health come from, and become complacent.

One of the truest sayings around recovery groups is, "You can't keep it if you don't give it away." The door to recovery is opened to you because others passed this way before. It is your joy, as well as your responsibility, to keep the door open for those who follow you, and lead them to the door if they can't find it. It is the only way to ensure that others get free from their secrets.

And To Practice These Principles In All Our Day-To-Day Living. Here is the most practical part of the Twelve Steps. Take what you have learned, and keep doing it every day. Practice admitting your powerlessness over the problems in your life. Practice acknowledging God's ability to run your life and keep you from practicing old behaviors. Practice new thinking and behavior skills. Practice prayer and meditation. Like the athlete who must exercise daily to stay in shape, you need to practice daily the new skills you have learned, so you can stay in good emotional and spiritual shape. It took many years of practicing old behaviors for you to end up with such low self esteem and such a lack of boundaries. It will take practice to become the new person you want to be. But it is possible!

Congratulations to all who embark on this journey of the Twelve Steps. These steps when followed are a tried and true path to end the secrets of your addiction, and become the woman you were truly destined to be. The addiction has attempted to thwart your process of reaching your destiny as a woman, and the lives you touch will be greater for the effort you make daily staying clean from your secrets.

Professional Helpers

In addition to the vital attendance and involvement in Twelve Step recovery, many female sex addicts benefit greatly from professional therapy.

The counselor telling me I was an addict started me on the road to recovery. I really wanted it for my kids and my husband, but now I want it for me and them. --Julie

Therapy has guided me to my recovery. --Constance

In our study of women sex addicts we asked several questions about therapy. Of the women in our study 87.5% stated that they went to therapy for their addiction issues. Only 12.5% stated that they did not seek professional help for their sexual addiction. The largest percentage of respondents (75%) found, that therapy in their recovery from sexual addiction was beneficial. Four percent stated that therapy was not helpful, and 21% stated that this did not apply to them.

Another question pertaining to therapy was if they felt that their sex addiction was minimized as they sought professional help. The response to this question was that 36% felt that their sex addiction was minimized by the professional they sought help from, but 64% felt that their problem with sexual addiction was not minimized by the professional they sought help from.

We asked whether the first therapist that they went to identified her as a sex addict. Unfortunately 64% reported that no, the first therapist did not identify her sex addiction, and 36% stated that their first therapist did identify them with sexual addiction.

How many hours of therapy went by until they were identified as sex addicts? The average response to the amount of hours may astound you. The average hours of therapy received, before being identified as a sex addict, was 138 hours.

Lastly, we asked those who have gone to therapy if a sexual advance had been made toward them. Their response was that 91% did NOT get propositioned for sex by their therapist. It is sad to report that 9% were asked by their therapist to have sex with them.

I have included this chapter to encourage you to find the right therapist to get your needs met, and to say that therapy can be a helpful and safe experience.

Similar to the medical or financial fields, the mental health field has various levels of professionally trained people. These professionals have a wide variety of philosophies and training perspectives, and can meet the various needs of women sex addicts.

Psychiatrist

Psychiatrists are medical doctors. They attend several years of medical school, and are trained to look at biological reasons for problems with the human being. They are trained in medications that influence the chemistry of the brain. This professional can be a valuable help and support to a female sex addict, if she has been previously diagnosed with a disorder of depression, manic-depression, bi-polar, or other problem that requires the supervision of a medical doctor. He or she can prescribe medication the sex addict might need to feel better, such as antidepressant medication.

If the psychiatrist has had addiction training, or has had exposure to workshops dealing with sexual addiction, he or she may be of more help to you as you work on your issues.

Psychologist

A psychologist is quite different from a psychiatrist, although they are often confused as they both have the designation of "doctor." Psychologists are Ph.D., Ed.D., or Psy.D.'s, not medical doctors. They have not attended and graduated from medical school. They are not licensed physicians. Therefore, they cannot prescribe medication. They spend their educational training looking at the cognitive, or thinking, aspects of the human being, such as Intelligence Quotient, reading and math levels, psychological testing, and the like. He or she is often trained to do individual, group, and marital therapy.

A psychologist with a doctorate in psychology can be of great help to the woman addicted to sex, especially if he or she has had experience working with sex addicts. A psychologist can be of help in therapy, especially if the addict is experiencing any psychological disorder such as depression, suicidal thoughts, or a compulsive eating, sleeping, alcohol disorder or sexual abuse, family of origin issues, etc. Often these survival mechanisms respond well to treatment under the care of a trained and licensed psychologist.

Licensed Professional Counselor

The Licensed Professional Counselor, or L.P.C., usually has either Masters level training, or Ph.D. level training with expertise in counseling or another field, i.e., sociology or anthropology. They can acquire a counselor's license through taking certain counseling classes. A Master's level degree is the minimum required for the L.P.C. in most states. The master's level professional may also have a degree in an area other than counseling, like an M.Ed. (Master's in Education), and take ten or fifteen classes in counseling during or after his or her graduate degree program, to acquire a professional license from the state he or she practices in. This is something to note in your initial interview with a Licensed Professional Counselor. You can ask exactly what their background is, because some licenses may not require a degree in counseling in some states. This can be important for the women sex addicts to know when they are seeking help for their own issues, or for the issues regarding their family, marriage, or children.

The Master's level L.P.C., much like a psychologist, can be a great resource for a sex addict as she deals with family and individual problems. An L.P.C. is usually able to identify and deal with depression, obsessive/compulsive disorders, addictive disorders, co-dependency, and other issues. L.P.C.'s, like psychiatrists and psychologists, have ongoing training and, in most states, will have a more reasonable fee structure for those seeking counseling. In finding a Licensed Professional Counselor, ask how many years they have been practicing, and review the "Questions to Ask" section at the end of this chapter, to determine the counselor's experience with sexual addiction treatment.

Social Workers

Social Workers will have either a Bachelor's or a Master's level education. They may have several levels of certification which can differ from state to state. They may be a Certified Social Worker (CSW) or a Masters Level Social Worker (MSSW), depending on their experience. Their training is mostly from a social perspective. Seeing issues from a social perspective is beneficial, and can be helpful, but unless specific training is given to the Social Worker in the field of addictions, there may be limits as to how helpful they can be.

However, if there is a need for social services for the family, or for the sex addict -- for example, in finding places for residential treatment -- a social worker can usually be quite resourceful. In some states the social worker is much like a Licensed Professional Counselor, as they provide individual, group, or family therapy. In other states and situations they may do social histories and things of that nature. In finding a social worker, you will need to find out what educational training and experience they have had. You may find that this will be a very beneficial relationship to you, as you seek help for either your own issues, or those of your family. Again, refer to the "Questions to Ask" section at the end of this chapter for further information.

Pastoral Counselors

Pastoral counseling is also available in many areas. Pastoral counselors include people who have professional degrees in counseling from an accredited seminary or institution. They may have a Doctoral level education (Ph.D.), or they may have a Master's level education. Pastors of local congregations would also be included in this category. Although most pastors minimally have a bachelor's level education, some may have no formal education at all. Such counselors can be significantly helpful to those who have strong church, Christian, or religious backgrounds. Pastoral counselors can be very helpful in your recovery, because development of spirituality is a significant part of recovery for the whole person.

The strengths of a pastoral counselor would include his spiritual training, coupled with professional experience, and professional training in the fields of addictions, or counseling and psychological training. With such training, a pastoral counselor could be of the utmost benefit.

Some possible weaknesses of the pastoral counselor might be a lack of training or skill in some areas. The pastor who has had no training in counseling may be of brief support to the female sex addict, but might not be as beneficial in resolving personal issues, or identifying other psychological problems that a sex addict might have. Pastors are usually not trained counselors but can be a great support to the woman in the recovery process of sexual addiction, as far as accountability. Some denominations have female pastors and female pastoral counselors. As a female you may find a female pastoral counselor more helpful to your individual support needs.

The pastoral counselor, like all other professionals discussed, should be asked the appropriate questions from the "Questions to Ask" section. This is very important. Often, their understanding of addictions and sexual issues can influence how therapeutic they can be to you.

Christian Counselors

Christian counseling is another form of counseling which is now readily available in most larger cities, as well as in some smaller communities. Christian counseling is not exactly the same as pastoral counseling. Many Christian counselors do not hold a position as a pastor, nor will they have professional pastoral counselor education training.

A Christian counselor is often professionally trained in the theory of counseling, psychology, and human development. These counselors can be Master's or Doctoral level trained professionals, but the training that the counselor receives can vary widely. It is wise to check the Christian counselor's training prior to having any therapeutic relationship.

There is a specific benefit in having a Christian counselor for those who embrace the Christian faith. They can be a great source of help, especially if they are able to integrate biblical truths and biblical understanding into the healing process. They can be very supportive and encouraging to the personal development of the female sex addict, and can also facilitate growth for the whole family. Again, ask the questions relating to training and expertise in the area of sex addiction. Just because they are a Christian does not guarantee they understand, or can successfully treat sex addiction.

Certified Alcohol and Drug Addiction Counselors or Licensed Chemical Dependency Counselors

CADAC's and LCDC's are available in most areas, although their designations may differ from state to state. These are counselors with a variety of training backgrounds. They may have a Ph.D., a Master's, or Bachelor's degree, or may have had no formal education whatsoever. Again, the training of an individual counselor is very significant.

This cannot be stressed more than in the field of alcohol and drug addictions. In some states individuals recovering from alcoholism or drug addiction, who want to enter the helping profession, find that such certification is the easiest way into this field. They do have a valid experience and understanding of the addiction process, as well as an understanding of the recovery process. However, caution must be used, in that recovering people often have multiple addiction problems. This is something to be noted when interviewing an addiction counselor.

In addition, it is important to ask how they have integrated a Twelve Step philosophy into their own lives. Unless a counselor has done at least a Fourth and Fifth Step and has begun the process of making amends, his or her perceptions might still be clouded by guilt and shame; and the counselor might not be able to facilitate the growth you need in your life.

Addiction counselors do have some strengths, however. They are often trained in family systems theory. They are familiar with the dynamics of addiction and usually come from a Twelve Step perspective. Often these counselors can be found working in alcohol and drug addiction treatment centers. Sometimes they share an office with a psychiatrist, psychologist, or Master's level counselor. They are often supervised in their work by a degreed professional. You can ask if the case load is being supervised, and by whom, and what that supervision process is. This is important because some supervisors, due to time constraints, will not review each case thoroughly. Another benefit to an addiction counselor is that he or she would be aware of recovery groups in the area, and the importance of support groups.

Marriage and Family Counselors

Marriage and family counselors can have a variety of degrees in education also. They may have a Ph.D., or a Master's degree in marriage and family counseling. For women who are sex addicts, this may or may not be helpful, depending on the situation. If you are in a marriage or a committed relationship, such a counselor can be very beneficial.

Marriage and family counselors come from a family systems approach, taking into consideration the needs of the entire family, and not just the needs of one person. Also, they will be highly attuned to how each family member processes problems, and how the family members interact with each other.

For example, in some addictive systems the addict is the one who is perceived as needing help, the spouse is the one who is strong and "helps" the addict, while the children are the supporters and cheerleaders in helping dad and mom. From a systems approach, a counselor might look at this situation and say, "Mom needs to be sick, so that dad can be a helper. Dad needs to give up the helper role and establish his own identity and boundaries, so that if Mom recovers, the family doesn't need somebody else to be sick, i.e., the children or Dad himself."

The marriage and family counselor will be highly astute in these matters and can be quite beneficial to the female sex addict, as well as to the family as a whole. Refer to the "Questions to Ask" section on the following page to determine what training and experience this counselor has in addictions in general, and in sexual addiction specifically, as well as in the recovery process from sexual addiction.

It is very appropriate to interview the professional you are considering as a therapist. Each addict has a different history, and could have possible conflicts with certain professionals due to their past experiences. Also, the many professionals discussed here represent a sort of continuum of care. At one point in your recovery one type of professional might be more helpful than another. Many practices include several types of therapists, and are able to treat sex addicts from what is known as a multi-disciplinary view. In interviewing a potential therapist, consider the following list of questions.

Sexual Recovery Therapist

A sexual recovery therapist (SRT) can be any of the above counselors you have read about so far in this chapter. They, however, have undergone specialized training to treat sexual addiction. These therapists have also been supervised by myself or someone trained by me. They would be able to help you though the various stages of your sexual addiction recovery. You can go to www.aasat.org and see if one of these specifically trained therapists are in your area. If not, utilize the below questions for a local therapist or read on about telephone counseling.

Questions to Ask

1. Do you have experience working with sex addicts?

2. How many sex addicts have you seen in the last two months?

3. Are you trained to do therapy with people with addictions? (State or Board Certification)

4. Are you a recovering person working a Twelve Step program?

5. What books have you read on sexual addiction?

6. Do you have specific training to deal with rape victims, and survivors of child sexual abuse, incest or other trauma? (If this applies to you)

Telephone Counseling

The current number of professionals who treat sex addiction specifically, and with a great deal of success, can be limited even in the larger metropolitan area. Heart to Heart Counseling Center has established telephone counseling for sex addicts, the partners of sex addicts, and couple counseling.

We have seen the same level of success for clients utilizing our telephone counseling as those who come in to our office. More information can be found at the back of this book on these services. This form of counseling is especially helpful for those who travel quite a bit, because they can call for their appointment from anywhere and speak to the same counselor every week. Telephone counseling is also helpful to those who feel that their confidentiality is of utmost importance. We see many physicians, lawyers, ministers, entrepreneurs, and students who don't want to run into their sex addiction counselor at the grocery store. They also don't have to walk into his or her office where they may be seen by someone they may know. Some like it also because they don't have to locate a baby-sitter to set up an appointment or leave the house. For whatever reason you may have for using the phone for counseling, it has been very successful for the recovery process.

Also offered for those not in the Colorado Springs, CO area is our 3-Day Intensive where you can get a significant amount of help in a relatively short period of time, without taking off of work for a long amount of time. You can read further about this popular method of help for your recovery in the appendix of this book also.

In this book you have taken a journey through the secrets of many women like yourself. You may have felt some of their pain in your own life as well. I strongly encourage you to take the next step of recovery for yourself. That may be attending a Twelve Step Support Group, getting further informed by reading more recovery related material, or calling a therapist. Whatever your next step is, take it! You really are worth living without the secret any longer. I wish for you the same freedom from your secrets that the women in this book have talked about and many others have taken.

Appendix

Feelings List

1. I feel (put word here) when (put a present situation when you feel this).
2. I first remember feeling (put the same feeling word here) when (explain earliest occurrence of this feeling).
Rules For Couples: 1- No examples about each other or the relationship. 2-Eye contact. 3-No feedback

Abandoned	Aware	Close	Deprived	Feisty
Abused	Awestruck	Cold	Deserted	Ferocious
Aching	Badgered	Comfortable	Desirable	Foolish
Accepted	Baited	Comforted	Desired	Forced
Accused	Bashful	Competent	Despair	Forceful
Accepting	Battered	Competitive	Despondent	Forgiven
Admired	Beaten	Complacent	Destroyed	Forgotten
Adored	Beautiful	Complete	Different	Free
Adventurous	Belligerent	Confident	Dirty	Friendly
Affectionate	Belittled	Confused	Disenchanted	Frightened
Agony	Bereaved	Considerate	Disgusted	Frustrated
Alienated	Betrayed	Consumed	Disinterested	Full
Aloof	Bewildered	Content	Dispirited	Funny
Aggravated	Blamed	Cool	Distressed	Furious
Agreeable	Blaming	Courageous	Distrustful	Gay
Aggressive	Bonded	Courteous	Distrusted	Generous
Alive	Bored	Coy	Disturbed	Grouchy
Alone	Bothered	Crabby	Dominated	Grumpy
Alluring	Brave	Cranky	Domineering	Hard
Amazed	Breathless	Crazy	Doomed	Harried
Amused	Bristling	Creative	Doubtful	Hassled
Angry	Broken-up	Critical	Dreadful	Healthy
Anguished	Bruised	Criticized	Eager	Helpful
Annoyed	Bubbly	Cross	Ecstatic	Helpless
Anxious	Burdened	Crushed	Edgy	Hesitant
Apart	Burned	Cuddly	Edified	High
Apathetic	Callous	Curious	Elated	Hollow
Apologetic	Calm	Cut	Embarrassed	Honest
Appreciated	Capable	Damned	Empowered	Hopeful
Appreciative	Captivated	Dangerous	Empty	Hopeless
Apprehensive	Carefree	Daring	Enraged	Horrified
Appropriate	Careful	Dead	Enraptured	Hostile
Approved	Careless	Deceived	Enthusiastic	Humiliated
Argumentative	Caring	Deceptive	Enticed	Hurried
Aroused	Cautious	Defensive	Esteemed	Hurt
Astonished	Certain	Delicate	Exasperated	Hyper
Assertive	Chased	Delighted	Excited	Ignorant
Attached	Cheated	Demeaned	Exhilarated	Joyous
Attacked	Cheerful	Demoralized	Exposed	Lively
Attentive	Childlike	Dependent	Fake	Lonely
Attractive	Choked Up	Depressed	Fascinated	Loose

Lost
Loving
Low
Lucky
Lustful
Mad
Maudlin
Malicious
Mean
Miserable
Misundertstood
Moody
Morose
Mournful
Mystified
Nasty
Nervous
Nice
Numb
Nurtured
Nuts
Obsessed
Offended
Open
Ornery
Out of control
Overcome
Overjoyed
Overpowered
Overwhelmed
Pampered
Panicked
Paralyzed
Paranoid
Patient
Peaceful
Pensive
Perceptive
Perturbed
Phony
Pleasant
Pleased
Positive
Powerless
Present
Precious
Pressured
Pretty
Proud

Pulled apart
Put down
Puzzled
Quarrelsome
Queer
Quiet
Raped
Ravished
Ravishing
Real
Refreshed
Regretful
Rejected
Rejuvenated
Rejecting
Relaxed
Relieved
Remarkable
Remembered
Removed
Repulsed
Repulsive
Resentful
Resistant
Responsible
Responsive
Repressed
Respected
Restless
Revolved
Riled
Rotten
Ruined
Sad
Safe
Satiated
Satisfied
Scared
Scolded
Scorned
Scrutinized
Secure
Seduced
Seductive
Self-centered
Self-conscious
Selfish
Separated
Sensuous

Sexy
Shattered
Shocked
Shot down
Shy
Sickened
Silly
Sincere
Sinking
Smart
Smothered
Smug
Sneaky
Snowed
Soft
Solid
Solitary
Sorry
Spacey
Special
Spiteful
Spontaneous
Squelched
Starved
Stiff
Stimulated
Stifled
Strangled
Strong
Stubborn
Stuck
Stunned
Stupid
Subdued
Submissive
Successful
Suffocated
Sure
Sweet
Sympathy
Tainted
Tearful
Tender
Tense
Terrific
Terrified
Thrilled
Ticked
Tickled

Tight
Timid
Tired
Tolerant
Tormented
Torn
Tortured
Touched
Trapped
Tremendous
Tricked
Trusted
Trustful
Trusting
Ugly
Unacceptable
Unapproachable
Unaware
Uncertain
Uncomfortable
Under control
Understanding
Understood
Undesirable
Unfriendly
Ungrateful
Unified
Unhappy
Unimpressed
Unsafe
Unstable
Upset
Uptight
Used
Useful
Useless
Unworthy
Validated
Valuable
Valued
Victorious
Violated
Violent
Voluptuous
Vulnerable
Warm
Wary
Weak
Whipped

Whole
Wicked
Wild
Willing
Wiped out
Wishful
Withdrawn
Wonderful
Worried
Worthy

Guideline #1:
No Examples
About Each Other

Guideline #2:
Maintain Eye
Contact

Guideline #3:
No Feedback

The Twelve Steps of Alcoholics Anonymous
Adapted for Sex Addicts

1. We admitted we were powerless over our sexual addiction, and that our lives had become unmanageable.

2. Came to believe that a Power greater than ourselves could restore us to sanity.

3. Made a decision to turn our will and our lives over to the care of God as we understood Him.

4. Made a searching and fearless moral inventory of ourselves.

5. Admitted to God, to ourselves, and to another human being the exact nature of our wrongs.

6. Were entirely ready to have God remove all these defects of character.

7. Humbly asked Him to remove our shortcomings.

8. Made a list of all people we had harmed, and became willing to make amends to them all.

9. Made direct amends to such people wherever possible, except when to do so would injure them or others.

10. Continued to take personal inventory, and when we were wrong, promptly admitted it.

11. Sought through prayer and meditation to improve our conscious contact with God as we understood Him, praying only for knowledge of His will for us and the power to carry that out.

12. Having had a spiritual awakening as the result of these steps, we tried to carry this message to others and to practice these principles in all our affairs.

MEN'S RECOVERY

CLEAN RESOURCES

Every Christian man is born into a sexual war. The enemy attacks the young, hoping to scar them permanently and leave them ruined. But your past is not enough to keep you from the enduringly clean life you want and deserve. $16.99

This journal is designed to be used in conjunction with the Clean book and the Clean DVD set. This set can be used individually or in a church small group or accountability group. $14.99

This DVD set exposes you to many tried and true spiritual truths with very practical applications. You and your church are about to take an amazing journey towards God's insights for your freedom. $29.99

LUST FREE RESOURCES

Every man can fight for and obtain a lust free lifestyle. Once you know how to stop lust, you will realize how weak lust really can be. God gave you the power to protect those you love from the ravages of lust for the rest of your life! It's time to take it back! $13.95

This DVD series walks you through how every man can fight for and obtain a lust free lifestyle. Once you know how to stop lust, you will realize how weak lust really can be. God gave you the power to protect those you love from the ravages of lust for the rest of your life! It's time to take it back! $23.95

STAY CONNECTED

5080 MARK DABLING BOULEVARD., COLORADO SPRINGS, COLORADO 80918 719.278.3708 HEART2HEART@XC.ORG

- LINKEDIN.COM/IN/DOUGLASWEISSPUD
- FACEBOOK.COM/DOUGLAS.WEISS.18
- TWITTER.COM/DRDOUGWEISS
- SOUNDCLOUD.COM/DRDOUGWEISS
- DRDOUGWEISS.COM/BLOG
- "DR. DOUGS TIPS" FROM APP STORE
- VIMEO.COM/DOUGLASWEISS
- YOUTUBE.COM/C/DOUGLASWEISS
- PINTEREST.COM/DOUGLASWEISS
- INSTAGRAM.COM/DRDOUGWEISS

SUBSCRIBE TO OUR WEEKLY NEWSLETTERS AT DRDOUGWEISS.COM

Dr. Doug's MARRIAGE TIPS   Dr. Doug's RECOVERY TIPS   Dr. Doug's PARTNER TIPS

OTHER RESOURCES

"Born for War" teaches practical tools to defeat these sexual landmines and offers scriptural truths that empower young men to desire successfulness in the war thrust upon them. $29.95

This 2 hour DVD helps single women ages 15-30, to successfully navigate through the season of dating. $29.95

This 2 Disc DVD Series is definitely nothing you have heard before. Dr. Weiss charts new territory as to the why for sexual purity. $29.95

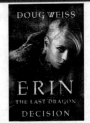

A gift for your daugher as she enters college. Letters to my Daughter includes my daily letters to my daughter during her first year of college. $14.95

Erin discovers she comes from a long line of dragons, dragons who have effectively maintained Earth's balance since the planet's beginning. Will she accept her fate and responsibility? $14.95

Within these pages of this book you will find a tried and true path for recovery from any addiction. Here you will get a biblical understanding to break the strongholds in your life forever. $22.95

This workbook provides tips, biblical principles, techniques, and assignments that Dr. Weiss has given his addicted clients with any addiction for over twenty-five years $39.95

These steps were derived from a Christian perspective and offer much needed insight and practical wisdom to help you get free and stay free from any addiction. $14.95

This Dvd series includes leadership training and fifty segments that are about 10 minutes in length. Churches of any size can begin a Recovery for Everyone group in their local church. $99.00

www.drdougweiss.com 719.278.3708

INTIMACY ANOREXIA

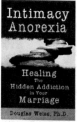

This hidden addiction is destroying so many marriages today. In your hands is the first antidote for a person or spouse with anorexia to turn the pages on this addiction process. $22.95

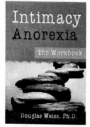

This is like therapy in a box. Inside is 100 exercises that have already been proven helpful in treating intimacy anorexia. $39.95

This is the only twelve step workbook just for intimacy anorexia. Each step gives you progress in your healing from intimacy anorexia. $14.95

This book will not only unlock the understanding of intimacy anorexia but you will also hear experiences of spouses who have found themselves married and alone. $14.95

This is the first workbook to offer practical suggestions and techniques to better navigate through recovery from your spouse's Intimacy Anorexia. $39.95

These Steps can further your healing and recovery from your spouse's Intimacy Anorexia. $14.95

This DVD will give you the characteristics, causes and strategies of intimacy anorexia. This DVD also provides solutions for the intimacy anorexic to start their road to recovery. $69.95

This DVD is for the spouse of an intimacy/sexual anorexic. Dr. Weiss will help you to start a journey of recovery from living with a spouse with intimacy anorexia. $49.95

WOMEN'S RECOVERY

This book offers the readers hope, along with a plan for recovery. Any woman who is a partner of a sex addict will find this book a necessity for her journey toward healing. $14.95

This is like therapy in a box for women who want to walk through the residual effects of being in a relationship with a sex addict. $39.95

This is an interactive workbook that allows the partners of sex addicts to gain insight and strength through working the Twelve Steps. $14.95

This DVD set is for any woman who is currently or was in a relationship with a sexual addict. If anger is still an issue, this material can help with her healing. $29.95

In this DVD set Dr. Weiss will expose the viewer to specific reasons as to why men lie and helpful strategies to end the lying. $44.95

In 90-minutes, this DVD answers the ten most frequently asked questions for partners of sex addicts. $69.95

This amazing DVD has 8 partners of sex addicts telling their stories through directed questions. A must DVD for every spouse of a sex addict. $19.95

This 2 hour DVD set was produced for divorced women who desire to date again. $29.95

www.drdougweiss.com 719.278.3708

MARRIAGE

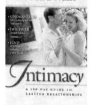

This 100 Day guide can transform couples from any level of intimacy to a lifestyle of satiation with their spouse. $11.99

In these pages you will walk with God as He creates the man, the woman and his masterpiece called marriage. $15.95

Dr. Weiss walks you through the creation and maintenance of your marriage.
Book 12.95/ DVD$29.95

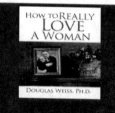

This book helps develop faithfulness, patience, forgiveness, service, respect, kindness, and celebration, all of which contribute to an exciting, loving and wonderful relationship. $13.99

By taking ten minutes a day to focus on each other, you can enhance your marriage in ways you'll appreciate for a lifetime. $14.99

In this 12 part DVD series, you will be exposed to tried and true principles to help you learn how to really love a woman. $69.00

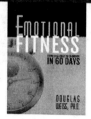

30-Day Marriage Makeover shows you how to energize your relationship and create the intimacy that you long for. $16.99

These DVD are a must for every Christian men and woman. You are practically and passionately walked through Christian sexuality that really works. $29.95(each)

Everyone has an unlimited number of emotions, but few have been trained to identify, choose, communicate, and master them. $16.95

COUNSELING

Counseling Sessions

Couples are helped through critical phases of disclosure moving into the process of recovery, and rebuilding trust in relationships. We have helped many couples rebuild their relationship and grasp and implement the necessary skills for an intimate relationship.

Individual counseling offers a personal treatment plan for successful healing in your life. In just one session a counselor can help you understand how you became stuck and how to move toward freedom.

Partners of sex addicts need an advocate. Feelings of fear, hurt, anger, betrayal, and grief require a compassionate, effective response. We provide that expert guidance and direction. We have helped many partners heal through sessions that get them answers to their many questions including: "How can I trust him again?"

A counseling session today can begin your personal journey toward healing.

3 and 5 Day Intensives

in Colorado Springs, Colorado
are available for the following issues:

- Sexual Addiction Couple or Individual
- Marriage Intensives
- Partners of Sexual Addicts
- Intimacy Anorexia
- Victims of Sexual Abuse
- Adult Children of Sex Addicts
- Teenage Children of Sex Addicts

Attendees of Intensives will receive:

- Personal attention from counselors who specialize in your area of need
- An understanding of how the addiction /anorexia and its consequences came into being
- Three appointments daily
- Daily assignments to increase the productiveness of these daily sessions
- Individuals get effective counseling to recover from the effects of sexual addiction, abuse and anorexia
- Addiction, abuse, anorexia issues are thoroughly addressed for couples and individuals. This includes the effects on the partner or family members of the addict, and how to rebuild intimacy toward a stronger relationship.

Partner's Recovery Training

Become a PRT®(Partner's Recovery Therapist) in the privacy of your own home or office. The days of traveling for conferences, supervision, and continuing education hours are over! You are in control of when and how long you take to complete your training. Watch and review your training DVDs as often as needed to gain valuable information and skills in treating partners of sexual addicts. This program is designed with the therapist in mind who works in an outpatient setting and needs practical information on treating partners of sexual addicts. Each participant will receive certification of completion suitable for framing after completing the training. This can be a great way to earn continuing education hours as well.

If you are currently certified by another organization to treat sexual addiction, this training will complement that training. Dr. Weiss developed this program utilizing his own proven methodology and modality, as well as his clinical application for treating partners of sexual addicts for over 25 years. With this AASAT training, you will gain proven clinical insight into treating the issues facing partners. You can be prepared! Over thirty hours of topics related to partners treatment are covered in this training, including:

- Partner Model
- Partner Grief
- Anger
- Boundaries
- Partners as Intimacy Anorexics

- Reactive Intimacy Anorexia
- Partner Worthlessness
- Polygraph Questions
- Separation
- Sex in Recovery

The Partner's Recovery Training course includes 31 DVDs and a workbook including bibliography.

For Just:$595.00
(that's less than$19.00 per hour!)